Kiln Theatre presents

HANDBAGGED
by Moira Buffini

September – October 2022 | Kiln Theatre

CAST

Actor 1
Romayne Andrews

Q
Marion Bailey

Actor 2
Richard Cant

Liz
Abigail Cruttenden

T
Kate Fahy

Mags
Naomi Frederick

CREATIVE TEAM

Writer
Moira Buffini

Director
Indhu Rubasingham

Designer
Richard Kent

Lighting Designer
Oliver Fenwick

Associate Lighting Designer
Nicki Brown

Sound Designer
Carolyn Downing

Associate Sound Designer
Sam Clarkson for Sound Quiet Time

Casting Director
Briony Barnett CDG

Voice & Dialect
Danièle Lydon

Wigs, Hair & Make-up Designer
Richard Mawbey

Co-Costume Supervisors
Megan Keegan-Pilmoor
Natasha Ward

Assistant Director
Dubheasa Lanipekun

PRODUCTION TEAM

Production Manager
Juli Fraire

Deputy Production Manager
Alysha Laviniere

Associate Production Manager
Jody Robinson

Company Stage Manager
EJ Saunders

Deputy Stage Manager
Cheryl Firth

Assistant Stage Manager (Book Cover)
Alex Jaouen

Technician/Lighting Operator
Eilidh MacKenzie

Wardrobe Manager
Maddie Bevan

Wigs Manager
Sophie Staples

Tech Swing
Kornelia Zielniewska

Production Carpenter
Tony Forrester

Lighting Programmer
Dan Haggerty

Set built by
Footprint and Kiln Theatre Workshop

KILN THEATRE ARE GRATEFUL FOR THE SUPPORT OF THE FOLLOWING FOR THIS PRODUCTION:

The Kiln Circle

AF076466

CAST

ROMAYNE ANDREWS
ACTOR 1

Theatre credits include: *Peter Pan Goes Wrong* (UK Tour); *Princess and the Hustler* (Bristol Old Vic & Hull Truck co-production); *Hamlet, King Lear, Cymbeline* (RSC); *A Fox on the Fairway* (Queen's Theatre, Hornchurch); *The Country Girls* (Chichester Festival Theatre); *Richard III* (Leeds Playhouse); *Unearthed, The Gift, Larksong, Mercian Hymns* (New Vic Theatre, Stoke).

Television and film credits include: *Doctors, Breeders.*

MARION BAILEY
Q

For Kiln/Tricycle: *Handbagged* (also West End), *The Arab Israeli Cookbook, Dance of Death.*

Theatre credits include: *The Deep Blue Sea, Blurred Lines, Grief, Black Snow, Man Beast and Virtue* (National Theatre); *A Kind of Alaska* (Bristol Old Vic); *Death of a Salesman* (Leeds Playhouse); *Mine, War and Peace, Kinder Transport* – TMA Awards Nomination (Shared Experience); *Incomplete and Random Acts of Kindness, Blest be the Tie, This is a Chair, Falkland Sound, Panic, Hush, Beside Herself* (Royal Court Theatre); *Holes in the Skin* (Chichester Festival Theatre); *Normal, All of You Mine* (Bush Theatre); *Cloud Nine* (The Old Vic).

Film credits include: *Brighton, Peterloo, Allied, Dead in a Week, Lady in the Van, Mr Turner* – Nomination, London Critics Circle Film Awards, *Toast, I'll Be There, Vera Drake, All or Nothing, Nasty Neighbours, Don't Get Me Started.*

Television film credits include: *Meantime, Sakharov, Way Upstream, Coppers, Persuasion.*

Television credits include: *All the Light We Cannot See, Damage, Shakespeare and Hathaway, The Dreamer, Endeavour, This is Going to Hurt, The Crown Series 3 and 4* – Screen Actors Guild Award Winner 2020 and 2021, *Temple, Britannia Series 2, SSGB, The Trials of Jimmy Rose, Case Histories, Him and Her, Being Human.*

In 1981 Marion was nominated Most Promising Newcomer in the Plays and Players Awards for Jackie in Mike Leigh's *Goose Pimples* at Hampstead Theatre & West End.

RICHARD CANT
ACTOR 2

For Kiln: *Wife.*

Theatre credits include: *Mr Gum and the Dancing Bear, The Normal Heart* (National Theatre); *Talent* (Crucible); *Henry Sixth Rebellion, Wars of The Roses, Maydays* (RSC); *After Edward, Edward II* (Shakespeare's Globe); *Saint Joan* (Donmar Warehouse); *Stella* (LIFT/Brighton Festival); *Medea* (Almeida Theatre); *My Night with Reg* (Donmar Warehouse/West End); *The Trial* (Young Vic Theatre); *War Horse* (West End); *Salome* (Headlong); *Troilus And Cressida, Cymbeline* (Cheek By Jowl).

Television credits include: *The Crown, It's A Sin, Silent Witness, Taboo, Mapp And Lucia, Outlander, Vexed, Above Suspicion – The Red Dahlia, Doctor Who, Bleak House, Midsomer Murders.*

Film credits include: *My Policeman* (Amazon); *Take Care* (BBC Films/ MrMr); *Mary, Queen of Scots, Stan And Ollie, Sparkle, Past, Present, Future Imperfect, The Lawless Heart.*

ABIGAIL CRUTTENDEN
LIZ

Theatre credits include: *Swive* (Shakespeare's Globe); *Black Chiffon* (Park Theatre); *Her Naked Skin* (Salisbury Playhouse); *An Enemy of the People*, *A Marvellous Year for Plums* (Chichester Festival Theatre); *Accolade* (St James' Theatre); *Drawing the Line, 55 Days* (Hampstead Theatre); *The Seagull* (Headlong); *Benefactors, The Crucible* (Sheffield Theatres); *When Did You Last See My Mother?* (Trafalgar Studios); *The Knot of the Heart* (Almeida Theatre); *Afterlife, Flight* (National Theatre); *The Importance of Being Earnest* (Birmingham Rep/The Old Vic); *Tartuffe* (Playhouse Theatre).

Television credits include: *Not Going Out* (as series regular Anna), *Fresh Meat, The Outcast, Benidorm* (as series regular Kate Weedon), *Sex and the City, Teenage Kicks, The Commander, Foyle's War, The Robinsons*.

Film credits include: *Munich: The Edge of War, Denial, Charlotte Gray, The Theory of Everything, Await Further Instructions, Hideous Kinky*.

KATE FAHY
T

Theatre credits include: Plays at Liverpool's Everyman Theatre, Royal Court Theatre, Young Vic Theatre, Hampstead Theatre, Orange Tree Theatre, National Theatre Studios and Kiln Theatre, including Edward Albee's *The Goat* at the Almeida Theatre and West End. She has played Margaret Thatcher (T) in *Handbagged* in New York, Washington and the UK tour.

Television credits include: *The Nearly Man, Poirot, The House of Elliot, Danton's Death, The Mozart Inquest, Oxbridge Blues, Silent Witness, The Suspicions of Mr. Whicher*. She is soon to be seen in ITV's *A Spy Among Friends* and Michael Winterbottom's *This Sceptered Isle*. She's best known on film for Joanna Hogg's *Archipelago*.

Directing credits include: Alexander Bodin Saphir's *Rosenbaum's Rescue* (Park Theatre); Jean-Claude Carriere's *Little Black Book* (Park Theatre); Oliver Cotton's *Wet Weather Cover* (Kings Head/Arts Theatre).

NAOMI FREDERICK
MAGS

For Kiln: *White Teeth*.

Theatre credits include: *Book of Dust* (Bridge Theatre); *Agnes Colander* (Theatre Royal Bath / Jermyn Street Theatre); *The Mentor* (Theatre Royal Bath / West End); *Hobson's Choice* (Theatre Royal Bath / West End); *As You Like It, The Heresy of Love* (Shakespeare's Globe); *Made in Dagenham* (West End); *Emil & The Detectives, Henry IV: Part 1 & 2* (National Theatre); *The Winslow Boy* (The Old Vic).

Naomi won Best Newcomer for her debut role as Carol in *Time & the Conways* (Manchester Royal Exchange), and she received recognition twice in the Ian Charleson Awards: for Isabella in *Measure for Measure* (Complicité at the National Theatre) and as Irina in *Three Sisters* (Nuffield Theatre / Theatre Royal Bath).

Television credits include: *Belgravia, EastEnders, Inspector George Gently, Casualty, Foyles War.*

Film credits include: *Father Christmas is Back, The Aftermath, The Children Act.*

Naomi read English at St Hilda's College, Oxford and trained at RADA.

CREATIVE TEAM

MOIRA BUFFINI
WRITER

For Kiln: *NW Trilogy*, *Handbagged* (also West End / UK tour / Washington / New York).

Theatre credits include: *Silence* (Birmingham Rep); *Manor* (National Theatre); *Gabriel* (Soho Theatre / UK tour); *wonder.land* (MIF / National Theatre); *Welcome to Thebes*, *A Vampire Story* (National Theatre); *Dying For It*, *Marianne Dreams* (Almeida Theatre); *Dinner* (RNT Loft / West End / UK tour); *Loveplay* (Barbican Theatre); *The Games Room* (Soho Theatre); *Blavatsky's Tower* (Machine Room).

Television credits include: *Harlots*, *Capital Lives*.

Film credits include: *Byzantium*, *The Dig*, *Jane Eyre*, *Tamara Drewe*.

INDHU RUBASINGHAM
DIRECTOR

Indhu Rubasingham is Artistic Director of Kiln Theatre. Her work for the company includes *The Wife of Willesden*, *The Invisible Hand*, *Pass Over*, *When the Crows Visit*, *Wife*, *White Teeth*, *Holy Sh!t*, *Red Velvet* (which transferred to New York and later to the Garrick Theatre as part of the Kenneth Branagh Season), *Handbagged* (winner of the Olivier Award for Outstanding Achievement in an Affiliate Theatre – also West End, UK tour, Washington, New York), *A Wolf in Snakeskin Shoes*, *Multitudes*, *The House That Will Not Stand*, *Paper Dolls*, *Women, Power and Politics*, *Stones in His Pockets*, *Detaining Justice*, *The Great Game: Afghanistan*, *Fabulation*, *Starstruck*.

Other theatre credits include: *The Father and the Assassin*, *The Great Wave*, *Ugly Lies the Bone*, *The Motherf**cker with the Hat* (Evening Standard Award for Best Play), *The Waiting Room* (National Theatre); *The Ramayana* (National Theatre/Birmingham Rep); *Belong*, *Disconnect*, *Free Outgoing*, *Lift Off*, *Clubland*, *The Crutch*, *Sugar Mummies* (Royal Court Theatre); *Ruined* (Almeida Theatre); *Yellowman*, *Anna in the Tropics* (Hampstead Theatre); *Secret Rapture*, *The Misanthrope* (Minerva, Chichester Festival Theatre); *Romeo and Juliet* (Chichester Festival Theatre); *Pure Gold* (Soho Theatre); *The No Boys Cricket Club*, *Party Girls* (Theatre Royal Stratford East); *Wuthering Heights* (Birmingham REP); *Heartbreak House* (Watford Palace Theatre); *Sugar Dollies*, *Shakuntala* (Gate Theatre); *A River Sutra* (Three Mill Island Studios); *Rhinoceros* (UC Davis, California); *A Doll's House* (Young Vic Theatre).

RICHARD KENT
DESIGNER

For Kiln/Tricycle: *Black Love*, *When the Crows Visit*, *Wife*, *Handbagged* (also UK tour / West End / Washington / New York), *Multitudes*, *The Colby Sisters of Pittsburgh, Pennsylvania*, *A Boy and his Soul*, *Paper Dolls*.

Theatre credits include: *Bad Jews* (Arts Theatre); *The Lodger* (Coronet); *My Cousin Rachel* (Theatre Royal Bath / UK tour); *This Is My Family* (Sheffield Crucible / Chichester Festival Theatre / UK tour); *The Mirror Crack'd* (Salisbury Playhouse, UK tour, NCPA India); *The Merchant of Venice + Julius Caesar* (Singapore Rep); *Man to Man* (Wales Millennium Centre, Wilton's Music Hall / BAM, NYC); *Dead Funny*, *The Mentalists* (West End); *Bad Jews* (Ustinov, St James Theatre, Arts Theatre, West End / UK tour); *Richard II* (Donmar Warehouse); *The Country Girls* (Chichester Festival Theatre); *Macbeth*, *Sheffield Mysteries* (Sheffield Crucible); *Winter's Tale*, *Cymbeline* (Shakespeare's Globe); *Anything Goes* (Sheffield Crucible / UK tour), *Oliver!* (Grange Park Opera); *Outside Mullingar* (Ustinov Bath); *Disco Pigs* (Trafalgar Studios 2 / Irish Rep

OLIVER FENWICK
LIGHTING DESIGNER

For Kiln/Tricycle: *The Invisible Hand, Pass Over, Holy Sh!t, White Teeth, Red Velvet* (also New York), *Paper Dolls, Handbagged* (also West End / UK tour).

Theatre credits include: *The Father and the Assassin, Tartuffe, The Great Wave, Ugly Lies the Bone, The Motherf*cker with the Hat, The Holy Rosenbergs, Happy Now* (National Theatre); *The Magician's Elephant, Love's Labor's Lost, Much Ado About Nothing, The Jew of Malta, Wendy and Peter Pan, The Winter's Tale, The Taming of the Shrew, Julius Caesar* (RSC); *Girls and Boys* (also New York), *Lela & Co, Routes, The Witness, Disconnect* (Royal Court Theatre); *Sweat, One Night in Miami, The Vote, Berenice* (Donmar Warehouse); *My City, Ruined* (Almeida Theatre); *The Sun, the Moon and the Stars* (Theatre Royal Stratford East); *Saved, A Midsummer Night's Dream* (Lyric Hammersmith); *To Kill a Mockingbird, Hobson's Choice, The Beggar's Opera* (Regent's Park Open Air Theatre); *A Number, Travels with My Aunt* (Menier Chocolate Factory); *Gloria, Occupational Hazards, Reasons to Be Happy, Private Lives* (Hampstead Theatre); *Calendar Girls* (UK tour); *Pride and Prejudice, Hamlet, The Caretaker* (Sheffield Crucible); *Oleanna, King Lear, Di, Viv and Rose, The Importance of Being Earnest, Bakersfield Mist, The Madness of George III, Ghosts* (West End).

CAROLYN DOWNING
SOUND DESIGNER

For Kiln/Tricycle: *The House That Will Not Stand, Handbagged* (also West End / UK tour).

Theatre credits include: *Death of a Salesman* (Young Vic Theatre); *All My Sons* (The Old Vic); *Downstate* (Steppenwolf Chicago / National Theatre); *Fiddler On The Roof* (Chichester Festival Theatre); *Mother Courage* (Royal Exchange Theatre); *A Woman of No Importance* (West End); *Coriolanus, Julius Caesar, Antony and Cleopatra, King John* (RSC); *House of Bernada Alba* (Royal Exchange); *Les Liaisons Dangereuses* (Broadway/Donmar Warehouse); *Fathers and Sons, Dimetos, Absurdia* (Donmar Warehouse); *As You Like It, Our Country's Good, The Motherf***er With The Hat, Dara, Protest Song, DoubleFeature* (National Theatre); *Chimerica* (Olivier Award – Best Sound Design); *Carmen Disruption, Blood Wedding, Summer and Smoke* (Almeida Theatre); *The Believers, Beautiful Burnout, Love Song* (Frantic Assembly); *Hope, The Pass, The Low Road, Choir Boy* (Royal Court Theatre); *All My Sons* (Schoenfeld Theater, NYC); *Angels in America* (Headlong); *Blue/Orange, Blackta, After Miss Julie* (Young Vic Theatre); *Thérèse Raquin* (Theatre Royal Bath); *Twelfth Night* (Sheffield Crucible); *Much Ado About Nothing, To Kill A Mockingbird* (Manchester Royal Exchange); *Kasimir & Karoline, Fanny och Alexander* (Malmö Stadsteater); *Tre Kronor* (Dramaten, Stockholm).

NICKI BROWN
ASSOCIATE LIGHTING DESIGNER

Nicki is Head of Production at Kiln Theatre.

Theatre credits include: As Associate Lighting Designer – *Yerma* (Young Vic Theatre / New York); *Cat on a Hot Tin Roof* (West End); *A View from the Bridge* (Young Vic Theatre / West End / Broadway / Chicago); *A Midsummer Night's Dream, Happy Days, The Changeling* (Young Vic Theatre); *Hedda Gabler* (National Theatre); *Lazarus* (King's Cross Theatre). As Lighting Designer – *Why It's Kicking Off Everywhere, Blackta, The Space Between, The Surplus, The Curtain, Two Endless Minutes* (Young Vic Theatre); *A Miracle, Gone Too Far!, Contractions, Fear & Misery / War & Peace, 93.2fm* [also UK tour] (Royal Court Theatre);

36 Phone Calls (Hampstead Theatre); *The Exquisite Corpse* (Southwark Playhouse / Wales Millennium Centre); *The Duke in the Darkness* (Tabard); *8 Women* (Southwark Playhouse); *Gutter Junky* (Riverside Studios); *Ours* (Finborough Theatre); *By Parties Unknown* (site specific); *The Elephant Man* (Union / Brazilian tour). As Assistant Lighting Designer – *Much Ado About Nothing* (The Old Vic).

SAM CLARKSON FOR SOUND QUIET TIME
ASSOCIATE SOUND DESIGNER

Theatre credits include: As Sound Designer – *Manic Street Creature* (Paines Plough Roundabout, Edinburgh Festival); *The Mr Thing Show* (Pleasance Dome, Edinburgh Festival); *The Pirate the Princess and the Platypus* (Polka Theatre); *An Evening of Eric and Ern* (The Lowry, Salford); *Glengarry Glen Ross* [also UK tour] (West End); *King Kong a Comedy* (The Vaults); *Mr Thing* (Arcola Theatre); *Murder Ballad* (Arts Theatre). As Associate Sound Designer – *Life of Pi* (West End); *Ich war noch niemals in New York* (Theatre de Westerns, Berlin). As Senior Production Sound Engineer – *Fantastically Great Women* (UK tour); *The Lion, the Witch and the Wardrobe* (UK tour) *Frozen, All About Eve, The Inheritance* (West End); *War Horse* (International tour); *Anastasia* (Japan); *9 to 5 the Musical* (UK tour); *The Curious Incident of the Dog in the Night-time* (West End / UK tour); *Appropriate* (Donmar Warehouse); *Caroline, or Change* (Hampstead Theatre); *Sweat* (Donmar Warehouse / West End).

Television credits include: *Looking a lot like Christmas* (A Donmar Festive Concert), *Potted Panto* (Amazon Stream), *Monster Court* (CBBC).

soundquiettime.com

BRIONY BARNETT CDG
CASTING DIRECTOR

For Kiln/Tricycle: *The Darkest Part of the Night, NW Trilogy, When the Crows Visit, White Teeth, Half God of Rainfall* (also Birmingham Rep), *Handbagged* (also West End), *The Invisible Hand, Ben Hur, A Wolf in Snakeskin Shoes, The House That Will Not Stand, The Colby Sisters, One Monkey Don't Stop No Show.*

Theatre credits include: *The Fellowship, The Memory of Water, The Death of a Black Man* (Hampstead Theatre); *Overflow, Chiaroscuro, An Adventure, The Trick* [also tour] (Bush Theatre); *An unfinished man* (Yard Theatre); *Princess and the Hustler* (Bristol Old Vic / tour), *Black Men Walking* (Scottish tour); *Again* (West End); *Abigail's Party* (Hull Truck); *Black Men Walking* (Manchester Royal Exchange / tour); *Fences* (West End / Theatre Royal Bath); *A Raisin in the Sun* (Sheffield Crucible / tour); *Ticking* (West End), *Play Mas* (Orange Tree Theatre).

Film credits include: *Bluebird, Samuel's Trousers, Bruce, Gypsy's Kiss, The Knot, High Tide, What We Did On Our Holiday* (children), *Common People, Tezz, Final Prayer, Love / Loss, Stop, A Sunny Morning, Value Life, Conversation Piece, 10by10.*

Television credits include: *Outnumbered* (children), *Just Around the Corner* (children), *Dickensian* (children), *Inside the Mind of Leonardo.*

DANIÈLE LYDON
VOICE & DIALECT

Danièle trained at Central School of Speech and Drama.

For Kiln: *Girl on an Altar, The Invisible Hand, White Teeth.*

Theatre includes: *Collaboration* (Young Vic Theatre); *The Mirror and the Light* (West End); *The Visit* (National Theatre); *All My Sons, Mood Music* (The Old Vic); *Harry Potter and the Cursed Child* (West End / Broadway / Melbourne); *School of Rock, The Lieutenant of Inishmore, Bat Out of Hell* (West End); *Billy Elliot* (West End / UK tour); *Big Fish, Sex With Strangers, Dry Powder, You and I* (Hampstead Theatre); *Twilight Zone* (Almeida); *Carousel* (ENO); *The Curious Incident of the Dog in the Night-Time, Medea, The Motherfu**er with the Hat, Man, Superman, The Visit, Treasure Island* (National Theatre).

Television includes: *The Hunt for Raoul Moat, House of the Dragon, The Lazarus*

Project, The Sandman, The English, Top Boy 4, Baptiste, Victoria, Poldark, Dark Angel, The Paradise, Vera, Boy Meets Girl, George Gently, An Inspector Calls.

Film includes: *Downton Abbey: A New Era, Death on the Nile, Shipbreakers, Where is Anne Frank?, Mercy, Life, Rogue One: A Star Wars Story, A United Kingdom.*

RICHARD MAWBEY
WIGS, HAIR & MAKE-UP DESIGNER

Theatre credits include: *Hairspray, Elf, Legally Blonde, The Producers, Guys and Dolls, End of the Rainbow, Waitress, Fiddler on the Roof, Joseph and his Amazing Technicolour Dreamcoat, Mrs. Henderson Presents, Merrily We Roll Along, White Christmas, Top Hat, 9 to 5 The Musical, The Lieutenant of Inishmore, Sweet Chartity, Madame de Sade, Frost/Nixon, Kiss Me Kate, Starlight Express, From Here to Eternity, Thoroughly Modern Millie, The Commitments, Pinter at the Pinter, The Libertine, Urinetown, The Ruling Class* (West End); *Assassins* (Menier Chocolate Factory).

Film credits include: *Titanic, Star Wars, The Hunt for Red October, Harry Potter and the Chamber of Secrets, It's De Lovely, Mask of Zorro, Disney's The Santa Clause.*

Television credits include: *Cilla, Little Britain, Poirot, Vikings, Dame Edna, Mr. Selfridge, Ripper Street, French and Saunders, The Catherine Tate Show, Gavin and Stacey, Larkrise to Candleford, Miss Marple, House of Saddam.*

DUBHEASA LANIPEKUN
ASSISTANT DIRECTOR

Training includes: For Directing – Sundance Institute and Adobe – Ignite Fellowship for Emerging Directors; Directors In Practice Programme (StoneCrabs Theatre); Young Vic Theatre Springboard [Jennifer Tang]; National Theatre Young Studio. For Writing – Ifeyinwa Frederick Scholarship, Soho Theatre's Writers Lab. For Dramaturgy – Script Panel (Royal Court Theatre); New Writing Coordinator (Warwick Rep Theatre Company). Other – TYTP (Talawa Theatre Company) [Ryan Calais Cameron]; We Are Parable's Momentum Talent Scheme with Channel 4 and 4Skills; Edinburgh TV Festival's The Network Talent Scheme.

Theatre credits include: As Director – *Bone* (Omnibus Theatre); *Deb & Joan* (The Canal Café Theatre); *Blind Date* (Katzpace); *A.I. in Wonderland* (University of Warwick). As Assistant Director – *WE NEED TO TALK ABOUT GRIEF* [R&D] (Donmar Warehouse); *I Know My Husband Loves Me* (The Union Theatre).

Film credits include: As Director – *Blue Corridor 15* (BBC, ICA, Dazed).

"Kiln Theatre has revitalised the cultural life of Brent and brings world-class theatre at an affordable price to people from all walks of life."
Zadie Smith

Kiln Theatre sits in the heart of Kilburn in Brent, a unique and culturally diverse area of London where over 140 languages are spoken. We are a welcoming and proudly local venue, with an internationally acclaimed programme of world and UK premieres. Our work presents the world through a variety of lenses, amplifying unheard / ignored voices into the mainstream, exploring and examining the threads of human connection that cross race, culture and identity.

"This place was a special cocoon. Now she has grown and blossomed into a beautiful butterfly." **Sharon D Clarke**

We believe that theatre is for all and want everyone to feel welcome and entitled to call the Kiln their own. We are committed to nurturing the talent of young people and our local communities, to provide a platform for their voices to be heard.

"I wanted to say thank you for creating the most diverse theatre I have been to. In terms of race, culture, class, age, everything – not only in the selection of shows and actors, but in the audience."
Audience member, 2021

Welcome to Kilburn.

Kiln Theatre
269 Kilburn High Road,
London, NW6 7JR

KilnTheatre.com

info@KilnTheatre.com

 @KilnTheatre

Registration No. 1396429. Registered Charity No. 276892

CREATIVE ENGAGEMENT AT KILN THEATRE

We create free projects; from workshops to performances to events with and for people who live, learn or work in Northwest London. Children, young people and adults from our local communities are encouraged to have fun, be inspired, aspire, and have their voices heard through connection, skills building and theatre making.

MINDING THE GAP AND SCHOOLS

Minding the Gap, our drama project for young people newly arrived in the UK, has been running for over 10 years. We work with local schools and colleges EAL departments to provide creative drama-based sessions, which aim to develop students' creativity, confidence and engagement in the arts.

We believe all young people should have access to arts and culture and are passionate about making sure our work is affordable and accessible to local schools. Our School's programme includes backstage workshops, Teacher's CPD, Resource Packs and bespoke projects which are co-designed with schools and until March 2023, we are able to offer each state Brent secondary school 30 free tickets.

YOUTH AND PATHWAYS

The Youth & Pathways programme aims to develop the next generation of artists and audiences. Through our Youth Theatres and Young Company, participants make friends, develop their confidence and theatre making skills through workshops and performing theatre and film productions.

We are committed to creating direct and transparent pathways into Kiln and out to the wider theatre ecology through work experience, placements and the Kiln Collaborators. Kiln Collaborators receive paid training in facilitation, leadership, theatre making and support the development of future young people's work.

COMMUNITIES

Our Communities work celebrates the unique, cultural and artistic life of our local area. We want to hear and advocate for the priorities of local residents, through co-creation of stories and theatre making. Upcoming activity includes tours, cinema screenings in partnership with local organisations, a Town Hall Talk produced in partnership with artist Linett Kamala, Monthly Masterclasses, community Kiln Collaborators, projects for elders and Listen Local Young Writers.

For more information about our work and how to get involved:

See our website **kilntheatre.com/creative-engagement** or email us on **getinvolved@kilntheatre.com** or WhatsApp us on **07375 532006**.

SUPPORT OUR WORK

As a charity, we rely on donations from our audience members and our community of supporters to achieve our mission: to make theatre for all.

We need your help to stage our internationally renowned, innovative productions, to offer a platform for people of all ages and backgrounds to express themselves, and to ensure our building is open as a welcoming hub for all. We want everyone to feel entitled to our space and to feel empowered by their engagement with us.

KILN CIRCLE

The Kiln Circle sits at the heart of our theatre. The Circle are given special opportunities to get close to the work on our stage and the artists involved in each of our seasons. Donations start from £2,500. For more information on joining this philanthropic supporters' group, contact Catherine Walker on **catherinewalker@kilntheatre.com** or **020 3946 8389**.

DONATIONS

Donations play a crucial role in enabling our work to continue. Join our community of supporters!

- Set up a regular donation from £3/month
- Join the Kiln Circle
- Attend one of our special fundraising events
- Name a seat in our auditorium
- Remember us in your will
- Set up a partnership through your company
- Introduce us to a trust or foundation

BECOME A SUPPORTER TODAY

www.kilntheatre.com/give
give@kilntheatre.com
020 7625 0132

Registered Charity No. 276892

Registered with FUNDRAISING REGULATOR

THANK YOU

We are so grateful to all our supporters, whose donations enable us to use the power of storytelling to champion unheard voices and to ensure that everyone can experience the power of theatre.

STATUTORY FUNDERS

Arts Council England

MAJOR DONORS AND KILN CIRCLE

Primrose and David Bell
Jules and Cheryl Burns
Sir Trevor and Lady Susan Chinn
Matthew Greenburgh and Helen Payne
Ros and Alan Haigh
Adam Kenwright
Jonathan Levy and Gabrielle Rifkind
Frances Magee
Dame Susie Sainsbury
Jon and NoraLee Sedmak
Christopher Yu

INDIVIDUALS

James Baer and Henry Chu
Laure Z. Duvoisin
Carol and Gary Fethke
Sue Fletcher
Atalanta Goulandris and Stephane Gripari
Betise Head
Nicola Horton and Tiffany Evans
Nazima Kadir and Karl Gorz
Elaine Morris
Richard Naylor
Ann and Peter Sprinz
Sarah and Joseph Zarfaty

TRUSTS AND FOUNDATIONS

29th May 1961 Charitable Trust
The Austin and Hope Pilkington Trust
Backstage Trust
BBC Children in Need
Bertha Foundation
Boris Karloff Charitable Foundation
Chapman Charitable Trust
City Bridge Trust
The D'Oyly Carte Charitable Trust
Esmée Fairbairn Foundation
Foyle Foundation
Garfield Weston Foundation
The Golsoncott Foundation
John Lyon's Charity
The John Thaw Foundation
Marie-Louise von Motesiczky Charitable Trust
Pears Foundation
The Richard Radcliffe Charitable Trust
The Roddick Foundation
The Royal Victoria Hall Foundation
Stanley Thomas Johnson Foundation
The Vanderbilt Family Foundation
Wellington Management UK Foundation
Young Londoners Fund

COMPANIES

Bloomberg Philanthropies
Synergy Vision

We are grateful to Arts Council England, DCMS and HM Treasury for our grant from the Culture Recovery Fund.

FOR KILN THEATRE

Artistic Director
Indhu Rubasingham

Executive Director
Daisy Heath

Associate Director
Amit Sharma

Associate Designer
Tom Piper

General Manager
Mirain Jones

Assistant General Manager
Robyn Bennett

New Work Associate
Tom Wright

Peggy Ramsay Foundation / Film 4 Awards Scheme Playwright in Residence
Amy Trigg

Assistant to the Artistic & the Executive Directors
Muriel de Palma

Box Office & Ticketing Manager
Spyros Kois

Assistant Box Office Manager
Mary Christensen

Box Office Team
Maria Koutsou
Jeremy Fowler
Fadi Giha
Gee Mumford
Trevor White

Cleaning Supervisor
Ragne Kaldoja

Cleaners
Theresa Desmond
Karina Haro
Jose Luz
Joslette Williamson

Head of Creative Engagement (Maternity Cover)
Romana Flello

Head of Creative Engagement (Maternity Leave)
Jenny Batt

Communities Manager
Maria Shury-Smith

Youth & Pathways Manager
Kyron Greenwood

Minding the Gap & Schools Manager
Juliet Styles

Youth & Community Placement
Catherine Moriarty

Finance Director
Sophie Norvill

Finance Manager
Felix Andrew

Interim Finance Support
Sophie Wells

Fundraising Director
Livvy Brinson

Fundraising Manager
Lynne McConway

Fundraising Manager
Catherine Walker

Fundraising Administrator
Caitlin Carr

Head of Marketing & Communications
Amy Thomas

Marketing Assistant
Alexandru Sones-Dawkins

Press Representative
Kate Morley PR

Head of Operations & Front of House
Simon Davis

Catering Manager
Angeliki Apostola

Audiences & Front of House Manager
Dana McMillan

Operations Administrator
Camille Wilhelm

Duty Managers
Sophia Capasso
Daniella Faircloth
Maya Tonkin

Catering Assistants
Hannah Carnac
Anne-Claire Le Comte
James Lloyd

Front of House Assistants
Isabelle Ajani
Iman Boujelouah
Asher Brandon
Saoirse Byrne
Jonah Garrett-Bannister
Katy Gore
Sophie Greaves
Lashay Green
Greg Higginson
Berlyn Jensen-Wallace
Felix Kai
Dami Laoye
Kirsty Liddell
Temi Majekodunmi
Eleanor Potter
Rawdat Quadri
Riley Reed
Jacqueline Reljic
Rosie Stancliffe
Laetitia Somé
Fizza Syed
Romario Williams

IT Consultant
Richard Lucas

Head of Production
Nicki Brown

Deputy Production Manager
Alysha Laviniere

Technical Events Manager
Dave Judd

Production Administrator
Aksa Saghir

Cinema Technician
Emmett Cruddas

Resident Assistant Designer
Pip Terry

Board of Trustees
Nicholas Basden
Louis Charalambous
Dominic Cooke CBE
Moyra McGarth Brown
Sita McIntosh (Chair)
Karen Napier
Shrina Shah
Zadie Smith
Christopher Yu

Handbagged

Moira Buffini's plays include *Blavatsky's Tower* (Machine Room), *Gabriel* (Soho Theatre), *Silence* (Birmingham Rep), *Loveplay* (Royal Shakespeare Company), *Dinner* (National Theatre and West End), *Dying for It*, adapted from *The Suicide* by Nikolai Erdman (Almeida), *A Vampire Story* (NT Connections), *Marianne Dreams* (Almeida), *Welcome to Thebes* (National Theatre), *Handbagged* (Tricycle Theatre and West End), *wonder.land* (National Theatre), *NW Trilogy* (Kiln Theatre) and *Manor* (National Theatre). Screenplays include *Jane Eyre*, *Tamara Drewe*, *Byzantium* and *The Dig*.

by the same author
from Faber

MOIRA BUFFINI: PLAYS ONE
(*Blavatsky's Tower, Gabriel, Silence, Loveplay*)

MOIRA BUFFINI: PLAYS TWO
(*Dinner, Dying for It, A Vampire Story, Welcome to Thebes, Handbagged*)

DINNER
DYING FOR IT
MARIANNE DREAMS
based on the novel by Catherine Storr
WELCOME TO THEBES
WONDER.LAND
MANOR

MOIRA BUFFINI

Handbagged

faber

First published in 2013
by Faber and Faber Limited
The Bindery, 51 Hatton Garden,
London EC1N 8HN

Reprinted with revisions 2022

Typeset by Brighton Gray
Printed and bound in the UK by CPI Group (Ltd), Croydon CR0 4YY

All rights reserved
© Moira Buffini, 2022

Moira Buffini is hereby identified as author
of this work in accordance with Section 77 of the
Copyright, Designs and Patents Act 1988

All rights whatsoever in this work, amateur or professional,
are strictly reserved. Applications for permission for any use
whatsoever including performance rights must be made in
advance, prior to any such proposed use,
to United Agents, 12–26 Lexington Street, London W1F 0LE

No performance may be given unless a licence
has first been obtained

This book is sold subject to the condition that it shall not,
by way of trade or otherwise, be lent, resold, hired out
or otherwise circulated without the publisher's prior consent
in any form of binding or cover other than that in which
it is published and without a similar condition including
this condition being imposed on the subsequent purchaser

A CIP record for this book
is available from the British Library

978-0-571-38142-5

Printed and bound in the UK on FSC® certified paper in line with our continuing
commitment to ethical business practices, sustainability and the environment.
For further information see faber.co.uk/environmental-policy

Our authorised representative in the EU for product safety is
Easy Access System Europe, Mustamäe tee 50, 10621 Tallinn, Estonia
gpsr.requests@easproject.com

6 8 10 9 7 5

For Susan Buffini
Bigger than both of them

*This play would not have been written
without the help and encouragement
of Indhu Rubasingham*

Handbagged is a fictional account that has been inspired by true events. Incidents, characters and timelines have been changed for dramatic purposes. Often, the words are those imagined by the author. The play should not be understood as biography or any other kind of factual account.

Handbagged was first performed at the Tricycle Theatre, London, on 26 September 2013. The cast, in alphabetical order, was as follows:

Q Marion Bailey
T Stella Gonet
Liz Clare Holman
Actor 1 Neet Mohan
Actor 2 Jeff Rawle
Mags Fenella Woolgar

Director Indhu Rubasingham
Designer Richard Kent
Lighting Designer Oliver Fenwick
Sound Designer Carolyn Downing

Handbagged was revived at the Kiln Theatre, London, on 9 September 2022. The cast, in alphabetical order, was as follows:

Actor 1 Romayne Andrews
Q Marion Bailey
Actor 2 Richard Cant
Liz Abigail Cruttenden
T Kate Fahy
Mags Naomi Frederick

Director Indhu Rubasingham
Designer Richard Kent
Lighting Designer Oliver Fenwick
Associate Lighting Designer Nicki Brown
Sound Designer Carolyn Downing
Associate Sound Designer Sam Clarkson
    for Sound Quiet Time
Casting Director Briony Barnett CDG
Voice & Dialect Danièle Lydon
Wigs, Hair & Make-up Designer Richard Mawbey
Co-Costume Supervisors Megan Keegan-Pilmoor,
    Natasha Ward
Assistant Director Dubheasa Lanipekun

Characters

T
an older Margaret Thatcher

Q
an older Queen Elizabeth II

Mags
a younger Margaret Thatcher

Liz
a younger Queen Elizabeth II

Actor 1
playing
A Palace Footman
Kenneth Kaunda
Nancy Reagan
Enoch Powell
Neil Kinnock
Michael Shea
Kenneth Clarke
A Protestor

Actor 2
playing
Denis Thatcher
Peter Carrington
Gerry Adams
Ronald Reagan
Michael Heseltine
Arthur Scargill
Rupert Murdoch
Geoffrey Howe
Prince Philip

HANDBAGGED

ONE: THOSE ARE PEARLS THAT WERE HER EYES

Enter Mrs Thatcher, elderly.

T　　Freedom
　　　Democracy
　　　They are things worth dying for.
　　　We must never
　　　Never stop resisting those who would take them from us
　　　And when they have been taken
　　　We will fight until we get them back.

　　　The act of resistance is our defining act as human beings.
　　　To say 'No, I will not stand for that,
　　　I will not collude, collaborate, negotiate
　　　I will not compromise'
　　　To say to the enemies of freedom 'You are wrong'
　　　To resist, whatever the cost

　　　To say No

　　　This is courage
　　　This is integrity.
　　　I would be proud if this word defined me:

　　　NO

　　　I'd like a chair
　　　I don't need one but I'd like one
　　　I will not ask for one
　　　If I wait, they will notice

　　　They will bring me one

　　　One of the men

Dancing around me in their suits
Ties flapping in the wind.
Holding their documents like babies
The men
I could pin them wriggling with my gaze
And then release them with a smile
I liked to do it
Girlish
I was girlish

Queen Elizabeth II enters dragging a chair. She is elderly.

Q   You look as if you need a chair

T   I'm quite capable of standing, thank you

Q   I'm bringing you a chair

T   There really isn't any need

The Queen places it.

Q   Here

T   No thank you

Q   I've gone and brought it now, sit down

T   Thank you, no

Pause.

Q   We conceive parliamentary institutions, with their free speech and respect for the rights of minorities, to be a precious part of our way of life and outlook. They inspire a broad tolerance in thought and expression.
During recent centuries, this message has been sustained and invigorated by the immense contribution, in language, literature and action, of the nations of our Commonwealth overseas. Our

Commonwealth gives expression, as I pray it always will, to living principles as sacred to the Crown and Monarchy as to its many Parliaments and Peoples. I ask you now to cherish them – and practise them too; then we can go forward together in peace, seeking justice and freedom for all men

T   Why don't you sit down?

Q   No thank you

Pause.

What can one say here?

Q   How far can one go?

T   Oh, don't hold back
It's all beyond our control

Q   Indeed

T   All artifice and sham

Q   I've never been fond of the theatre

T   No

Q   We once saw *War Horse*
We liked the horses

T   One would like to speak frankly

Q   One doesn't want to blab

T   Oh no, there's nothing worse than a blabber
We have never blabbed

Q   Whatever we say must stay between these three walls

T   Nothing uncontrolled
No outpouring

Q	Then we'd better have some tea.
	When one needs to control the pouring
	Tea can be most reassuring

TWO: MAY THE FOURTH BE WITH YOU

A younger Queen (Liz) and a younger Thatcher (Mags) enter.

Mags	We knew we had won by the early hours of May the fourth. Finchley roared with jubilation
	Maggie
	Maggie
	Hours later it was still thundering in my ears
Liz	Philip and I had put money on the result
Q	No we had not
Liz	He was sure the lady would carry the day.
	I thought the nation might baulk at a female PM
T	I can remember an odd sense of loneliness when I received the call, which summoned me to the palace
Mags	The audience, at which one receives the Queen's authority to form a government, comes only once in a lifetime. When one is re-elected, one doesn't go. So that first meeting is unique
Liz	She was my eighth
Q	Winston, Sir Anthony,
Liz	Harold M, Sir Alec
Q	Dear Harold W
Liz	Heath –

Q	And Jim Callaghan. He bade me farewell that morning
Liz	It is affecting when they go
	One doesn't have time to turn around
Out goes the last and in comes the next with barely a pause
	And one has often built up a relationship
Mags	My feelings on the way to the palace –
T	I wasn't thinking about feelings
I was thinking there is so much to do.
	I wanted to get behind that desk in Number 10 and get doing
Mags	My teeth ached from smiling
And as we drove through the palace gates
I felt almost lifted off the ground
As if the hands of fate
T	I wasn't sentimental
Mags	Were holding me
	And words were coming to me from my childhood, from our chapel.
I wanted to
T	I didn't
Mags	I wanted to give thanks
Liz	It wasn't the first time I'd met Mrs Thatcher, but this was different. Meeting one's PM is like
Like meeting the other side of the coin
We are both Britain
T	I never said 'there is no such thing as society'
Q	Yes you did. It was in *Woman's Own*

T	I said there is a living tapestry of men and women
Q	You said 'Who is society? There is no such thing' and then you repeated it
T	I said the beauty of that tapestry will depend upon how much each of us is prepared to take responsibility for ourselves
Q	Society is the people
T	Society is a framework for freedom Freedom that gives a man room to breathe To make his own decisions and to chart his own course There is the individual And there is family. There is no such thing as –
Q	No such thing as Britain That's how you sounded
T	It's the idea that the State is society that I reject
Q	Didn't the war teach us that we're all in this together? One wants the people to be looked after
Mags	I found the monarch's attitude
Liz	I found the Prime Minister's attitude
Mags	Towards the working of government
Liz	Towards the working of monarchy

Mags *and* **Liz**
    Absolutely correct

Footman
    I am a Palace Footman and I'll be leading the Prime Minister silently and respectfully to Her Majesty the Queen

Mags	One enters a different world at the palace
T	Everything is hushed
Footman	I am a functionary whose purpose is to serve To do my job well is to be unnoticed You may be interested to know that I have a City and Guilds Diploma in Butlering, and that the Royal Household is committed to Equality, Diversity and Inclusion
Q	Thank you for mentioning that We're quite modern you see
Footman	Prime Minister, the formal kissing of hands –
Mags	I know all the protocol. You don't need to tell me a thing
T	Denis was with me
Mags	I need Denis
T	I want Denis
Mags	Where's Denis?
Denis	(*entering*) Denis Thatcher, MBE Met the Boss at a function in Dartford Rattled along with her ever since. Recently retired from the board of Burmah Oil I'm an honest to God right-winger and I don't care who knows it
Mags	Denis
Denis	Always been a fan of Prince Philip Big, big admirer Leader of the pack in this male consort lark; Absolute model – thought I'd ask him for some tips

	I reckoned after years and years of PMs' wives,
	He might be grateful for a chap like me
T	Denis came to the door with me
Mags	Why do I suddenly feel like I'm back at school?
Denis	Come on, Boss
	You'll get on like a house on fire; bound to
	Just be yourself
Mags	I always am, dear. What a silly thing to say

Mags curtsies, deeply. She holds it, frozen.

Liz	With my previous Prime Ministers
	There was a gallantry
	A mutual letting down of hair
Q	Goodness gracious what a curtsy
Liz	They were all older than me and each in his own way quite charming.
	One always hopes for a confidante

Mags finishes her curtsy.

Liz	Congratulations on your victory, Prime Minister
Mags	Thank you, Your Majesty
T	She's ever so small
Q	She colours her hair
T	We're the same age
Q	Of the same era
	Formed in the war
T	In every way, we are peers

Mags kisses Liz's hand.

Liz	Britain's first female leader
	You must be feeling very pleased

T	Of course I don't notice I'm a woman
	I regard myself as Prime Minister
Mags	I always say if you want something said, ask a man
	But if you want something done ask a woman
Liz	Couldn't agree more
Q	My father never let Prime Ministers sit down
Liz	Please take a seat

They sit.

Q	We met every week for all the years she was in power
T	Our meetings were private
Liz	We never took notes
Mags	We are the only two who know what was said
Q	Of course stories about clashes
T	Nonsense
Liz	There was never any question
Mags	Stories about clashes
Q	We have got on very well with all of our Prime Ministers
Liz	I was very taken with your prayer on the steps of Number 10
Mags	Oh yes, St Francis
T	I said

T *and* **Mags**
> Where there is discord, may we bring harmony
> Where there is error, may we bring truth
> Where there is doubt, may we bring faith

Liz	Are you hoping the Conservatives will bring harmony? Because truth and faith are tricky things to supply
Q	I didn't say that. I said
Liz	What a crush there was on the steps of Number 10
Mags	Yes
Liz	Journalists and policemen are always so big One finds them enormous They rather crowded you I thought
Mags	Yes, they rather did
Liz	Yet you kept your self-possession
Mags	I am used to the hustle and the bustle
Liz	It'll only get hustlier And bustlier I'm sure
Mags	I shall relish it. I've lived the life of politics since I was twenty-five
Liz	You were a scientist before that?
Mags	First scientist to be PM
Liz	You really are a pioneer
Mags	I was a research chemist for Lyons Developing methods to preserve ice cream And make it fluffier I worked on Mr Whippy Which led the way with hydrogenated fats. Have you heard of it?
Liz	No
Mags	I am of course a barrister as well I qualified four months after my twins were born

Liz	Good gracious
Mags	So between the party, law, twins and cooking Denis breakfast I have always been very busy
Liz	I am genuinely in awe. I never even went to school
Mags	No
Liz	Your voice changed On the television When they asked about your father
Mags	Well I owe him everything I really do
Liz	One's father shapes one, doesn't he?
Q	I was interested in her family's shop
Mags	It was a very modest home Of course everyone knew deprivation in the war
Liz	Oh yes
Q	I'd done some discreet asking around
	And her mother, Beatrice – Methodist, terribly devout – Was the daughter of a cloakroom attendant. I thought that was an interesting fact
Mags	My father was very careful with money
	He abhorred debt – and I have that too
Liz	Your mother must have worked very hard
Mags	Oh yes but of course she was far more domestic. And after I turned fifteen, I had nothing to say to her
Q	Goodness
Liz	I still can't get my mother off the phone

Mags	My father took me out to council meetings and debates He was passionate about politics and about education
Q	Where did she get that accent?
Mags	When I got to Oxford and saw what was being taught – Somerville was very Left and I knew I wouldn't fit in – Something in me thought No, this is wrong, this is wrong No, these consensus economics cap profit You see what we have now is a failed socialist experiment
Q	Everything she said slipped into lecturing mode It was a feature of her conversation
Mags	Socialism
T	Socialism
Mags	Socialism is inimical to freedom. The left-wing slide we have been on leads inexorably to poverty and human bondage
Liz	I'm not a proponent, Prime Minister, but isn't the purpose of socialism to bring people out of poverty?
T	How wonderful; to enter into discourse with her
Mags	Have you read Friedrich Hayek's *The Road to Serfdom*, Ma'am?
Liz	No
Mags	He talks about the trend towards socialism as being a break with the whole evolution of western civilisation

Liz	Really
Mags	You see, our civilisation has grown from foundations of liberty and individuality laid down by the Christians and the Greeks. This individuality is our inheritance. Socialist centralised planning / is a negative to human development. The only way to build a decent world is to improve the level of wealth via the activities of free markets. My father knew this
Q	I'm afraid I 'tuned out' – as Charles would say –
	And when I tuned back in she was talking about her father again
Mags	He taught me that you've got to sell your goods every day
	It's a constant battle that's never won
	It's those who sell who will lift us out of poverty
Liz	I see
T	I wasn't sure Her Majesty had understood
Q	Her certainty was quite extreme
Liz	I wonder if Number 10 will be like that
Mags	How do you mean?
Liz	Like living above the shop
Mags	Oh yes. I'm sure I shall feel very much at home

Pause.

Liz Prime Minister
One likes to know what's going on
One likes to feel that one's a sort of sponge
You can come and tell me things
And some things stay

| | And some go out the other ear
One might occasionally do some good
And one can put one's point of view |
|------|---|
| Mags | This is such an honour |
| Liz | One is unelected, yes
But one is experienced |
| T | Disraeli stood in this very room and gave the Suez Canal to Victoria |
| Liz | And perhaps because one cannot publicly express opinion
One can be a trusted tool
Especially abroad |
| T | Churchill stood here with her father as the war raged around them |
| Liz | One's perhaps like an emollient
One sometimes smoothes the way. |
| T | And now me |
| Liz | One cherishes one's service |
| Mags | Yes, the weight of the cup in the hand
The shape of the handle, just so – is it Spode? |
| Q | My God, she hadn't listened |
| Liz | It's rather an everyday service I think |
| T | You have no idea what it meant for me
Meeting you on such an equal footing |
Liz	Will you be bringing any pets to Number 10?
Q	I thought if she's got a dog we've got a subject
Mags	I believe there is a cat
Q	There was no letting down of hair with her

T	You are my Queen I am your subject The first move towards a close relationship Could not have come from me
Mags	You never made it
Q	You didn't hear it
Liz	You hadn't listened
Denis	Margaret had always adored the Queen, absolutely revered her. We stood in the crowd cheering at her coronation. Seemed sad to me she came out so deflated
T	On my way back to Number 10 A thought stayed there insistently Despite my every effort to dispel it
Denis	Felt a bit like the grocer's daughter did you, love?
Mags	Not at all I felt as soon as I had left the room Her Majesty would shake me off – with a laugh
Liz	You're quite wrong
Q	There was nothing remotely funny about you
T	I had worked so hard for my achievements Her Majesty's were birthrights
Q	I have to accept that here I am And this is my fate
T	Fate has nothing to do with me It is all discipline and enterprise

THREE: SPANKING

Liz   I notice the Prime Minister didn't eat the biscuits. Let's try her with a sponge next time

Q   Ridiculous

Footman
     Very good, Ma'am

Q   An Audience is a working meeting and we don't serve cake

Footman
     May I ask you a question?

Q and Liz allow it.

     Is it different because this Prime Minister is a woman?

Liz   It is different because this Prime Minister is Mrs Thatcher

Footman
     (*to T and Mags*) Prime Minister, may I ask you a question?

T   Of course you may

Footman
     When you said that socialism was inimical to freedom, what did you mean?

T   I meant that

Mags   Socialism is the philosophy of failure, the creed of ignorance, and the gospel of envy. Its inherent virtue is the equal sharing of misery

T   Winston Churchill said that and I agree with every word

Mags	One cannot have liberty without economic liberty and we shall attain it with our monetarist policies and our strong stance against the trade unions. May I offer you our manifesto?
Footman	Thank you. Don't you think we need to hear something about the other side?
Mags	They lost
T	They are utterly discredited and that is thanks to me
Footman	Only there's a generation that don't know what they did
T	Yes, aren't you lucky?
Footman	But didn't the other side give Britain free health care, and sickness benefit and pensions?
Mags	May we push on?
Denis	Prince Philip and I House on fire But Margaret was struggling
Mags	Your Majesty, I have a query A slightly awkward one About our wardrobe It has occurred to me that when we attend the same event, our outfits may present complications For example, one wouldn't want to wear a similar colour or a clashing one
Liz	I never notice what anyone else wears
Mags	One wouldn't like to upstage

Liz	I shouldn't worry about that

Pause.

Mags	Do you have a lady, Your Majesty One of your ladies That perhaps my lady could speak to?
Q	The way she said 'Your Majesty' grated. Why couldn't she just call me Ma'am?
Liz	I have Bobo Bobo organises all my clothes
Mags	I have Crawfie Crawfie does everything for me She turns me out every morning looking spanking. Would it be acceptable if Crawfie were to ask Bobo? . . .
Footman	The butler who trained me has worked in the palace for thirty-five years. He said you overheard all sorts of things and that your job is to forget them. Then he told me some of the things he'd forgotten. The Queen used to call Mrs Thatcher 'that bloody woman'
Q	No one from the palace ever said that
T	Yes they did You and your sister did You think things didn't get back to Number 10 But I heard everything I knew exactly what you thought of me

The Queen ignores her, shaking invisible hands.

Q	One has so many people to meet So much to do
T	I never held an unkind thought about you I am your most loyal subject

Q	How do you do? Yes, community service is so important
T	Do me the courtesy of listening, please
Q	Two mayors? How lovely
Mags	The Queen is a continuum A line drawn through time From the dawn of England to the present day Her family symbolises all that is perfect and proper in British life She is
Liz	Completely useless That's the impression one got She thought we were fit for nothing more than shaking hands
Q	Oh, Barbados? Terribly nice place
T	I felt a tremendous desire to protect the Queen
Liz	One had been patronised before of course But it was worse being patronised by Mrs Thatcher
Q	A hairdresser, really?

FOUR: DANCING AT LUSAKA

Liz	I soon gave her proof of my usefulness. Rhodesia –
Q	Now Zimbabwe –
Liz	Had been a thorn in our side for fifteen years
Footman	Shall I fill them in on the history, Ma'am?
Liz	Do you have to? I don't want this to get dull and there's a lot to get through before the interval

T	We don't need an interval
Q	What?
T	I'd like to go right through
Q	But I enjoy the interval Sometimes it's the best part of the play
Liz	In my opinion, the people of Rhodesia deserve a fair election
Mags	In my opinion, the existing government of Rhodesia, whatever its flaws, is the only one that won't ruin the country
T	It was our first real disagreement
Q	Of course it wasn't. We never disagreed

Footman
 The young people might need the background, Ma'am. I can cover it in a sentence or two

Q Oh very well

Footman
 Rhodesia – now Zimbabwe – was ruled by a White minority led by Ian Smith. It refused to hold fair elections and there had been an escalating guerrilla war for several years as a result. The Zimbabwean Patriotic Front was led by the hugely popular Robert Mugabe, who was currently harboured by neighbouring country, Zambia

Q	Thank you. Very concise
Liz	The people deserve democracy
Mags	The Zimbabwean Patriotic Front is Marxist. Marxists do not respect democracy
Denis	I knew Rhodesia very well from my days at Burmah Oil. And if the blackies got in, the whole

	place would go down the bloody plughole. And with it, a great hairball of British interests and British trade
Liz	The Heads of Commonwealth conference is in Lusaka this year
Footman	Lusaka is the capital of Zambia
Liz	I think it's an ideal opportunity for us to get all the parties round the table
T	*Us?* Is the Queen suddenly a member of Her Majesty's Government?
Mags	Your Majesty, your government has grave concerns for your safety in Lusaka. We strongly advise you not to go
Liz	You advise me not to go?
Mags	It has been bombed. It is unsafe
Liz	I have only ever missed one Heads of Commonwealth meeting and that's because I was having Andrew
Mags	Your Majesty, Kenneth Kaunda of Zambia is thick as thieves with Mugabe and the guerrillas. / It is dangerous
Liz	We've known Kenneth Kaunda for years – he wouldn't let anything happen to me
Mags	Your government is responsible for your safety; you must let your government decide
Liz	So you are *telling* the monarch not to go?
Mags	I am merely trying to protect you, Your Majesty
Q	We were jolly well going

Liz	And if anyone tries to stop us there'll be a whole song and dance about it I can tell you
T	Of course, if the Queen wanted to go then the Queen had to go and all the security had to be provided
Q	You were the one who needed protecting You were too green to see it I knew I could be useful To you and to Britain So obviously I was going

Footman

    Would it be helpful if I changed parts now, Ma'am?
    I could stop being Palace Footman
    And play Kenneth Kaunda, President of Zambia

Q   Can you do that?

Footman

    Yes, I'll just go and prepare
    And when I come back, I will be him

    Actor 2 smoothly changes his glasses.

Carrington

    Prepare? I'm Peter Carrington, Foreign Secretary

    Actor 1 exits.

T   You're not Peter Carrington

Carrington

    Yes, for the moment I am

T   You're Denis

Carrington

    Yes I was, but now I'm Peter Carrington

T   How can you be Peter Carrington when you're Denis?

Carrington
>I'm representing Peter Carrington
>
>Just for a moment or two

T   Why?

Carrington
>Because I'm responsible for the Lancaster House Agreement. It gave Zimbabwe peace and democracy

T   Are you Denis or not?

Actor 2   No, I'm not

T   How dare you
How dare you attempt to impersonate him

T exits.

Actor 2   Look I'm playing several roles here – I mean, some of them have only got one line and others are horrible, thin caricatures but times are hard and it's a job. I don't want to offend anyone. All right? I am currently Foreign Secretary and Minister for Overseas Development; Peter, Sixth Baron Carrington

Q   He goes on to be Secretary General of NATO

Liz   Such a gentleman, Peter

Mags   Yes, you hail from the days when the Conservative Party was run by men from Eton

Carrington
>Of course you change all that – for a while

Mags   What if I want you to be Denis again?

Actor 2   I am employed to be anyone you need

Mags   Thank you. I shall go and make that clear

She exits.

Q	I have always loved Africa.
Liz	My first trip abroad was to South Africa
Q	I can honestly say it was one of the happiest times of my life
Liz	It was just after the war and there was such a feeling of hope and renewal in the air. There were picnics and big game hunts
Q	On my twenty-first birthday I made a speech

Carrington
    Ma'am, no one who heard it will ever forget

Q	I felt the whole Empire was listening
Mags	(*entering, with T*) Come on Peter. We're going to Lusaka
Liz	'I declare before you all, that my whole life, whether it be long or short, shall be devoted to your service and the service of our great Imperial family, to which we all belong . . .'

Carrington
    It was most affecting
    To hear the young princess
    Take on that great burden
    With such a sweet pure voice

T	There's a whole generation of men, Peter among them, who went through the war and are quite batty about the Queen

Carrington
    We would have lain down our lives for her –

Mags	Are you coming, Peter?

Carrington
    And still would

Mags	Peter – I'm already on the plane
Kaunda	(*entering*) I'm Kenneth Kaunda, Father of Zambia
Q	That's very good
Kaunda	I'm about halfway through my twenty-seven years of irreproachable rule, during which time I campaign tirelessly against White minority governments. I'm a giant of African politics. When we Commonwealth heads of government meet, we have equal status under the Queen. In other words, the British government is just one of many
T	Oh for the days of Empire
Kaunda	The Queen is like a mother confessor to us all A very down-to-earth person Always asking her incisive questions Really, she is an icon
Q	I arrived in Lusaka before Mrs Thatcher. I was determined to smooth her way
Liz	Kenneth, I want to know all about the Zimbabwean Patriotic Front. You let them train here; you give them arms – what are they like?
Kaunda	Her Majesty never wastes time
Liz	What about this Mugabe chap? I'm hearing such conflicting things
Kaunda	You know you can trust my opinion, Ma'am
Mags	On the plane, I was sick with dread
Carrington	Margaret, the Americans support free elections. The UN supports free elections. Frankly, our position is becoming untenable
Mags	But I cannot back down. This is my first outing on the international stage and –

Carrington
    And you can be seen to be listening

Mags   Peter, when one knows one is right, that is very hard

Carrington
    The thing that people forget is how cautious Margaret was
    She was very careful
    And she was persuadable
    In the early years at least

T   By the end of the flight my address was written

Mags   I should like to make it clear that the British government is wholly committed to genuine Black majority rule in Rhodesia

Carrington
    Zimbabwe

Mags   Zimbabwe

Q   Thanks to Peter, the lady had turned

Carrington
    Margaret put on a large pair of dark glasses
    I said what on earth are those for?

Mags   I am absolutely certain that when I land at Lusaka they are going to throw acid in my face

Kaunda   Welcome to Lusaka, Prime Minister
    I'm sure you will find it a very convivial place

Liz   I had taken Kenneth aside
    I told him you'd be nervous
    Pointed out that you were new

Kaunda   I have great love and respect for Britain's Queen. So I made her Prime Minister welcome. And in spite of everything I'd heard, I found the Iron Lady quite conversable

Mags	It turned out that Kenneth Kaunda was not as black as he'd been painted
Q	Did you really say that?
T	Yes, what of it?

Carrington
Margaret's speech was very well received. With British support, a free Zimbabwe was on the agenda

Kaunda	The atmosphere at the final reception was quite extraordinary
Liz	My work behind the scenes paid off Mrs Thatcher was accepted by the African leaders And I swear she began to enjoy herself
Mags	Crawfie had packed something special and I thought well by golly, I'm going to make a splash
T	No I didn't
Kaunda	Mrs Thatcher's dress was a dramatic shade of lime with a pineapple motif. Her blonde hair shone through the crowd Margaret, may I have this dance?

They dance.

Q	Denis was overheard asking the New Zealand High Commissioner
Denis	What do you think those fuzzy-wuzzies are up to?
Liz	I made it known I was available for a dance. Safest to have him talk about nothing

Denis and Liz are dancing.

Denis	The Queen certainly kept her cool in the tropical heat

Liz	Not quite the Gay Gordons, is it?
Mags	And so Rhodesia expired and Zimbabwe was born
T	The atmosphere was very special at Lusaka And that was due to the Queen
Q	Twenty-three years later she publicly expressed her gratitude
Kaunda	I'm being forgotten here. My diplomacy brought all the parties to the table
T	I doubt if that's what history will say
Denis	You brought it off – by dancing with Kaunda
Mags	I've always loved to dance. We had American servicemen in Grantham during the war. They were so glamorous
Liz	Oh yes
Mags	And I begged and begged to go dancing. My father wouldn't hear of it
Liz	We crept out on VE Day, my sister and I, with some officers we were friendly with; went into the crowd incognito – dancing on the street
Mags	Did you really?
Liz	Of course they recognised us. But the crowd was lovely
T	I was deeply gratified when she shared things with me
Mags	I cried when they brought down the Union Jack in Rhodesia
Liz	Did you?
Mags	I thought 'the poor Queen . . .'

Liz	Why?
Mags	Doesn't it grieve you? The demise of the Empire?
Liz	The Commonwealth is our solace. And all its nations are there by choice
T	I felt pain for Britain's decline To see how low we'd sunk in the world's esteem
Q	Not everything was in decline Child poverty was becoming a thing of the past
T	We were an economic snail An international nonentity
Q	Society had never been more equal
Mags	Someone had to stop the rot

FIVE: BOMBS I

T	If I had my way, Irish citizens in the UK would lose their right to vote and they'd be subject to the same immigration laws as everybody else
Mags	I never said that
T	But crikey I thought it
Q	Mrs Thatcher had lost her friend and mentor Airey Neave in an IRA bomb blast just before she was elected
Mags	He was one of freedom's warriors. No one knew how great a man he was except those nearest to him We must not let the people who got him triumph
Liz	Her voice cracked as she spoke of him

T	We had barely been back from Lusaka a week when the IRA murdered eighteen of Our Boys at Warrenpoint in a hideous ambush
Mags	At the security briefing one of the officers presented me with a torn epaulette. I said what is this? It was all that remained of his friend
T	Carnage
Liz	On the same day, at his home in Sligo, our cousin Louis Mountbatten –
Q	Dickie to those who knew him –
Liz	Set off with his family in his boat, the *Shadow Five*
Adams	Gerry Adams, Sinn Fein. What the IRA did to Mountbatten is what Mountbatten had been doing all his life to other people; and with his war record I don't think he could have objected to dying in what was clearly a war situation. He knew what he was doing, coming to our country. In my opinion, the IRA achieved its objective: people started paying attention to what was happening in Ireland
Q	The explosion was violent in the extreme.
	It was heard across the bay over two miles away Nothing but flotsam remained of the *Shadow Five*
Liz	It was terrible for Philip in particular Dickie was his uncle Had been like a father to him
Q	Two children died in that blast Boys aged fourteen and fifteen
Liz	You didn't phone me
Q	She didn't phone

Mags	Because I was new you see and I didn't know whether one telephoned the Queen or not Normally, you go through the system
Q	Members of my family had died
Liz	And I had to phone you
T	Of course I went to Ulster straight away And I got doing
Mags	We put a thousand more men in the RUC
T	I never ever compromised with terror I told them compromise? That is out
Mags	That is out
T	That is out I wanted troops on every street
Mags	I would root out
T	I would vanquish
Mags	Crush
T	Pulverise the IRA
Mags	And if they protest
T	If they protest
Ron	The ten most dangerous words in the English language are 'Hi, I'm from the government, and I'm here to help'
Mags *and* T	Ron
Q	One has seen many presidents come and go And from this peculiar position One can see that power rests in the office
Liz	Not in the individual

SIX: THE REAGANS ARE COMING

Ron There were two guys in Moscow waiting in line for vodka and one them says 'This line is too long; I've had enough. I'm going into the Kremlin and I'm going to kill Brezhnev.' So off he goes and after about an hour he comes back. And the other guy says, 'So did you kill him?' and he says 'No, that line was even longer.'

T Ron was even funnier than Denis

Mags The first time I set eyes on Ronald Reagan

T Apart from on the screen of course

Mags Was in the Royal Albert Hall in 1969.
There was the governor of California
Speaking as if it were just to me

Ron We're at war with the most dangerous enemy that has ever faced mankind in his long climb from the swamp to the stars;
Communism

Mags I knew in an instant that here was a visionary.
Not only that

T He was gorgeous
I'm sorry but why not say it?

Mags Never said it, never thought it

T Who can deny it? Not even Denis

Ron Someone once said to me 'How can an actor be president?' I said 'How can a president not be an actor?'

Q Have we seen any of his films?

Liz *The Cattle Queen of Montana*, that was one of his

Q	Oh yes, we liked that
Liz	We liked the horses
Mags	Long before he was elected, I used to cherish copies of his speeches in my bag –
Ron	Ladies and gentlemen, this is my wife
Nancy	Hello, how do you do? I'm Nancy Reagan
Mags	The First Lady
Nancy	We first met Maggie and Denis back when Ron was fighting for his nomination And those two? They hit it off straight away
Ron	She had a lot of spunk
Mags	We'd talk half the night about the dangers of big government
Nancy	They even had a conversation that went something like Wouldn't it be great if we two ruled the world? And then lo and behold A few years later
T	I was the first foreign leader to visit him in Washington after his inauguration
Liz	No you weren't. The Koreans were
Mags	We in Britain stand with you
T	America's successes will be our successes
Mags	Your problems will be our problems
T	And when you look for friends we will be there
Ron	In a dangerous world, one element goes without question: Britain and America stand side by side

Mags   We must be free or die who speak the tongue that Shakespeare spake

Ron   Margaret, I believe a real friendship exits between us

Mags *and* **T**
    So do I, Ron

Nancy   Dinner at the British embassy was a warm and beautiful occasion
Bob Hope was there; all sorts of wonderful people

Liz   I hear she's notoriously brittle

Mags   Who?

Liz   The First Lady

Mags   She's very slim, yes

Liz   Apparently it's her hustling that's propelled him into the White House – and now that she's there, I've heard she's knocking down walls and throwing out all the china

Q   I love gossip

Mags   She is undertaking some refurbishments

Q   Why wouldn't you gossip?
You knew I wasn't going to tell anyone

Liz   Well I would have told Philip

Q   And my sister

Liz   And probably Mummy and Anne

Mags   The First Lady adores the President
She's always at his side
I'm sure he relies on her

Liz   I heard she sees an astrologer about absolutely everything. One of these people who won't get their hair cut unless the moon's in the right place

Mags	We haven't discussed astrology, Your Majesty
Q	Oh it was such hard work
Liz	Do you not feel it's a bit of a performance with them? They are both actors you know
Ron	When I got shot in March '81, Margaret's letter of concern was top of the pile
Nancy	I cannot describe what I went through on that day
Ron	You don't have to, Nancy
Nancy	Yes I do, Ronnie. Because people need to know. A crazy man called John Hinckley, was obsessed with a teenaged actress called Jodie Foster – I'm not kidding – and he thought he would please her somehow, if he shot my husband. He let off six bullets
Ron	He was a lousy shot. Only one of them got me
Nancy	It stopped in his lung, an inch away from his heart
Ron	I was a lucky man. The surgeons who operated on me were all Republicans
Mags	His wit, even in such adversity. That showed real mettle
Q	Because of the shooting, the President was unable to attend Charles and Diana's wedding that summer
Nancy	I wasn't going to let him travel
Q	But luckily the First Lady came
Nancy	It was a fairytale event. Diana was so beautiful And no one does a Royal occasion like the British I missed Ronnie terribly
T	Yes, we all did

Nancy	I was in London five days and I had eighteen different engagements
Q	One of them was a polo match She came to meet Charles and Diana
Nancy	He was such a delightful, earnest young man And I could see even then that Diana had a stunning personality This was the romance of all times
Liz	I'd driven there in my jeep Headscarf on Mrs Reagan arrived in a cavalcade – of how many cars?
T	Six
Mags	One just for her hats I think
Liz	Really, Mrs Thatcher, was that a joke?
Mags	No
Liz	It was – you were being funny
Mags	It just slipped out
Q	She actually made a joke. It was a first. I thought she had no sense of humour whatsoever
Mags	I didn't mean anything. I admire the First Lady
Liz	But you've got to admit that the sixth car was a bit much
Mags	Thank goodness for such a lovely wedding, Your Majesty It's transformed a horrible summer

SEVEN: THE GUNS OF BRIXTON

Ron Nancy must have hit it off with Queen Elizabeth because that winter, we received an official invitation to Windsor Castle. No US president had ever stayed there before

Actor 1 I'm sorry but is that it about the summer of '81?

T I beg your pardon?

Actor 1 Are we moving on from the summer of '81?

Mags Yes

Actor 1 You don't want to mention the riots?

T No

Actor 1 The riots that flared up all over the country?

Q Oh, one found them very distressing and one said so in one's Christmas message

Actor 1 Massive civil unrest boiled over into insurrections against systemic racism and soaring unemployment: Brixton, Toxteth, Handsworth, Leeds, Manchester, Bradford, Portsmouth – to name but a few. They even rioted in High Wycombe

T You're Nancy Reagan

Mags Nancy Reagan was never concerned with unlawful rioting in British cities, I can assure you of that

Q May I refer you to my Christmas message? My feelings are made very clear

Actor 1 I just feel there's some massive omissions here –
The huge job losses; unemployment leapt by a million in one year
The criminalisation of Black youth
The unrest in Northern Ireland

	You can't skip the hunger strikes –
Actor 2	Look – it's not our gig, okay?
Actor 1	But they aren't telling the story
Actor 2	It's their story. That's the contract
Actor 1	I'm just saying that if you miss out the riots and all the unrest, people – you know, like younger people – might think nothing else happened in 1981 apart from the royal wedding and Nancy's hats
Liz	One was very concerned
Q	One's Christmas message is the only major speech of the year that is written without government intervention
Liz	This Christmas, we should remember especially the people of Northern Ireland who are attempting to live ordinary lives in times of strain and conflict; the unemployed who are trying to maintain their self-respect without work and to care for their families; and those from other parts of the Commonwealth who have come to Britain to make new lives but have not yet found themselves fully accepted
Actor 1	That must have really shaken things up
Q	Listen
Liz	Governments now regard it as their duty to try to protect their people, through social services, from the worst effects of illness, bereavement, joblessness and disability
Q	How much clearer could I have made things?
Actor 1	Maybe a bit clearer
Actor 2	Look, I don't think you should be disrespectful

	Constitutionally she's not allowed to state her opinions

Actor 1   I'm not being disrespectful
          I'm just pointing out that in the midst of all that Diana wedding stuff
          The whole country was boiling with rage

Mags   The whole country?
          The whole country?

Actor 1   Well, people on the street

Mags   Which people on the street?

Actor 1   There were crowds in every inner city

Mags   How many? How many in each crowd?

Actor 1   Well, in Brixton there was about five thousand

Mags   Five thousand yobs? – The whole country?

T   (*to the actors*) I'd like to remind you what you're here for and whose company you're in. Her Majesty was shot at during the Trooping of the Colour, two weeks before the Prince of Wales' wedding and did she go on about it?
          No she did not
          She passed it by without a word
          Such is her dignity
          Such is her courage

Q   One doesn't want to be standing here all night

Mags   We choose what is spoken about here and if you don't like it you can get on your bike

          Pause.

Actor 1   There was unprecedented strife. It should be marked, that's all. But in a stroke of casting genius, I've been asked to play Nancy Reagan

Mags	I fell over myself to be useful to Ron I would give him my careful advice at any hour of the day or night
Ron	Margaret certainly never held back with her advice
T	I would have guided his finger as it hovered over NATO's button I'd have made sure he held firm
Mags	But the first time I really needed him He let me down
Q	Can we skip this bit?
T	Pardon?
Q	We've been here aeons and we're not even through your first term
T	Your Majesty, how can you even suggest it?

EIGHT: ISLANDS IN THE STREAM

Ron	When Al Haig told me that Argentina had invaded the Falkland Islands, I said where in the name of ding-dong are they?
Nancy	No he didn't
Ron	A little ice-cold bunch of land down in the South Atlantic, of no strategic value to anyone
Nancy	He did say that
Mags	On the 2nd of April 1982 Argentina, led by General Galtieri and his Junta –
Q	We're not going through the whole thing, are we?
Liz	We don't need a blow-by-blow account
T	I'm sorry?

Q	It's been gone over again and again in all sorts of other places and I don't want to trudge through it here
Mags	Three days later, With UN approval A task force set sail from Portsmouth
Q	She's ignoring me
Mags	There would be no negotiation till these bullies had got off
Q	Did you see that?
T	That's when Ron should have stepped up
Q	Totally ignoring me
Mags	He should have said I support you one hundred per cent We are side by side This invasion of British soil is an outrage against democracy
Q	She's just going to carry on, isn't she? I might as well not be here
T	Ron sat on the fence When I needed him most
Mags	He sent a jetlagged proposal Suggesting we negotiate
T	Negotiate, with a tinpot dictator? I said No
Mags	No, Ron
T	Absolutely not
Mags	You're asking me to lie down And let naked aggression walk all over me I am not a doormat

	And you may not wipe your feet
Nancy	I think you Brits forget how close we are to Latin America
Ron	We'd spent time and money down there, funding anti-Communists – and Galtieri was no Communist
Liz	May I interrupt you for a moment? I was directly involved in the South Atlantic war First, as head of the Armed Forces
T	Oh yes
Liz	Then, as sovereign of the country that was being invaded
T	Yes of course, but that's all titular, isn't it?
Liz	And I was mother of a combatant. My son Andrew was out there
Q	Terribly brave
Liz	Your cabinet tried to give him a desk job But I insisted, insisted that he went Countless other mothers were waving off their sons Why should I be spared?
T	We were very grateful for your sacrifice
Mags	It was a battle of good over evil
Ron	Margaret, you've got to try the diplomatic initiative
Mags	I had an absolute clarity of purpose I knew I had to hold my nerve
T	And I was put, by Ron, on an equal footing with the Junta
Ron	We decided in the end on a pro-UK tilt

Mags	A tilt
T	Ron came through with a tilt
Mags	I felt personally let down
Q	You'd think Wouldn't you That she did the whole thing by herself That there was no one else involved
Liz	Well Andrew was on the HMS *Invincible*
Q	Quite heroic
Liz	And I can tell you there were a lot of people involved
Mags	I was stricken at our losses They caused me acute distress I wrote personally to the families of all the men who died
Liz	There it is again – I, me, I
T	This is all about taking the salute, isn't it?
Q	Nonsense
T	This is because when it was over I took the salute and not you
Q	I have kept silent on that subject, always
Ron	We could see that a certain amount of damage had been done to our special relationship
Q	So thank heavens for me
Liz	When the Reagans visited Windsor, the conflict was still at its height
Nancy	The Queen was so thoughtful She showed us up to our room herself

| | And you should have seen the little things she'd put out for us
There were letters from Abraham Lincoln
There was a note from George the Third saying 'America is lost to us!' |
|---|---|
| **Ron** | I found that very poignant |
| **Nancy** | And there was the sweetest letter from Her Majesty's parents, written when they were visiting President Roosevelt. It described a picnic they'd been on, where the King had eaten a hot dog for the first time in his life |
| **Liz** | For the only time in his life |
| **Nancy** | I was knocked out by Windsor Castle |
| **Liz** | Yes that's rather the idea |
| **Mags** | The battle for Goose Green was raging |
| **Ron** | The Queen had suggested we have a ride.
Now, I was worried, I can tell you;
At home in Santa Barbara I'd just pull on some jeans
And leap on, you know, John Wayne style – |
Mags	There was vicious hand-to-hand fighting on Mount Tumbledown –
Ron	But the last thing I wanted to come over as, was a cowboy –
T	They sank the *Atlantic Conveyor* –
Mags	I was existing on one or two hours' sleep
T	I felt intensely, intensely alive
Nancy	We wrote to the palace and asked what the President should wear

Liz	Boots, breeches and a sweater No need to be formal
Nancy	In the end we decided on something Old Hollywood Beautiful sports jacket over an open-necked shirt
Liz	We rode Burmese, our favourite
Nancy	Ron looked so elegant So did the Queen, in a charming headscarf
Ron	You know, she was in charge of that animal
Q	One was used to seeing photographers, but my goodness over a thousand I think
Liz	Those images were beamed around the world From Moscow to Buenos Aires
Q	Britain and America side by side in perfect harmony
Liz	The benefits of a good ride
Mags	Of course, the important thing about Ron's visit was his speech to parliament, when he talked about putting Marxism on the ash-heap of history
Q	No one remembers that
T	Four days later The Union Jack was flying over Port Stanley Right had prevailed Victory was ours
Mags	Enoch Powell stood up in the house and he said:

Pause.

Actor 2   That's you

Actor 1   No it's not

Actor 2   Yes it is

Actor 1	I made sure at the audition; I don't have to do it. Enoch Powell was sacked from the Tory front bench for his incendiary racist views. He thought it was clever to talk in Latin and he called Black children piccaninnies
Mags	Enoch Powell stood up in the house and he said
Actor 1	I'm not doing it
Mags	I beg your pardon?
Actor 1	I'm just not
T	Then you're very poor value for money
Mags	If you don't want this job
Actor 1	I do
Mags	Then I suggest you get on with it
Actor 1	He also refused to issue a warning about Thalidomide, which caused physical deformities in unborn babies, even when it was known to be dangerous. Fun fact
T	Enoch said
Powell	Her substance is ferrous metal of the highest quality Of exceptional tensile strength Resistant to wear and tear Usable for all national purposes
T	The Iron Lady had triumphed
Mags	I agree with everything the gentleman has said
Q	Gloriana, the papers called her Boadicea in pearls
Liz	I'd spent those weeks Along with countless other mothers

	Agonising for the safety of my favourite son –
Q	I have no favourites
T	All right, I took the salute It was my war It felt right at the time and Our Boys wanted it They wanted me I had brought them safely home Restoring Britain's honour and your flag

Pause.

Mags	It's done If I'd known you'd be this upset I'd have
Liz	You'd have what, Prime Minister?
Mags	I know my son wasn't out there but the following year when Mark got lost in the desert and I didn't know where he was for four whole days, I got an inkling of what you must have felt

Pause.

Mags	Are you freezing me out?

Liz is silent.

T	She froze me out for weeks over that salute
Q	Nonsense

NINE: COAL NOT DOLE

Liz	The following year we visited the Reagans in California
T	I won the next election with a landslide
Q	California please

Ron We invited Queen Elizabeth to our home, Rancho del Cielo

Nancy We threw them a Hollywood dinner. We invited movie stars; Julie Andrews was there, Rod Stewart sang

Ron I figured she'd like a ride, American style
And where better to provide it?

Mags If Ronald Reagan knew
If he knew what I really thought of him
His lazy intellect,
His mawkish sentiment
His floundering with briefs
It would damage our interests irrevocably

T On one thing, Ron was clear

Mags The evil of socialism

T I held on to that one thing

Mags I brought him Gorbachev
I gave Ron the Soviet empire in a golf cart

T To anyone who says that my diplomacy was poor I give them this: we ended Communism. The Iron Curtain is no more

Actor 1 Excuse me

Mags The first time I met Mikhail Gorbachev, I knew this was a man we could do business with

Actor 1 What year are we in?

T He came to power in 1985

Actor 1 Are you going to miss out the government's decision to allow America to site its cruise missiles on British soil?

Mags Yes

Actor 1 What about the women protesting at Greenham Common? –

Mags Eurgh

Actor 1 Or the huge CND marches?

Mags They weren't huge

Actor 1 What about the miners' strike? Are you going to miss that out too?

T I'd be glad to talk about the miners' strike. Let's talk about the miners' strike

Mags The power of the unions had to be destroyed. They were our next enemy

T I knew that if we crushed the miners, the whole trade union movement could be swept out of our way

Mags Where's Michael Heseltine? He was useful

Heseltine I'm Michael Heseltine. Most handsome member of the cabinet

Mags Hezza

Heseltine The most meticulous planning had been put in place. We'd been stockpiling coal for years. Arthur Scargill, militant leader of the miners union, was teased on to the worst battle plan at the worst possible time for him –

Mags We announced twelve pit closures in the spring, when nobody needed his coal

T We planned it like a military campaign

Mags We had to fight the enemy without in the

	Falklands. But the enemy within is more difficult And more dangerous to liberty
Liz	Have you ever been down a mine, Mrs Thatcher? I have I thought it was a dark and dangerous place to work I was deeply impressed by the men who laboured there. I've spoken with a lot of miners and their wives –
Mags	Then you are very knowledgeable –
Liz	And never, at any time Have I found them to be The enemy within
Actor 1	There was huge public support for the miners
Mags	They're behaving as a mob And we have no choice but to treat them as a mob
Liz	You're deploying my police force like an army
Q	There were pitched battles, brutal fighting, terrible casualties on both sides
Liz	The police stood side by side with the miners during the war and it upsets me how you have divided them
Mags	I have not divided them. Arthur Scargill has divided them
Actor 2	Shall I be Scargill?
Mags *and* **T**	No
T	The only helpful thing that Arthur Scargill ever did was neglect to hold a strike ballot. That was very helpful. Very helpful indeed

Mags	It revealed his undemocratic soul
Scargill	We've had riot shields, we've had riot gear, we've had police on horseback charging into our people; we've had people hit with truncheons and people kicked to the ground
Mags	You are stepping over the mark
Scargill	The intimidation and the brutality that has been displayed are something of a Latin American state
Mags	(*to Scargill*) He is the dictator He is the general
Liz	Neither would back down an inch
Q	When one thinks about it, they were very similar
Liz	I felt particularly sorry for the miners' wives, as the strike dragged through the winter
Mags	It is up to the miners' wives to tell the miners to be sensible
Actor 1	Did you really say that?
Mags	No husband of mine would have gone around shaming the country in that lawless way; picketing here, rioting there
Actor 1	But people were fighting for their livelihoods
Q	It was a whole year of strife
Mags	I welcome strife I welcome it In the cause of making Britain great again
T	That strike changed Britain forever
Q	Yes, we lost the feeling that had persisted since the war. We were no longer all in it together

Liz	In the end, the miners were beaten
Mags	We had won a stunning victory
Liz	Some of the wives handed them carnations at the pit gates as they returned to work; a flower which symbolises the hero. I thought that rather affecting
T	We had liberated industry
Actor 2	The miners' strike caused hatreds and divisions that have never healed and workers' rights have been eroded ever since. It was a tragedy; it was heartbreaking
Mags	Who's opinion is that?
T	Is that your own private opinion?
Actor 2	Yes
Mags	It is. It's his own opinion Would you tell me whose opinion these people have paid good money to hear?
Actor 2	Her Majesty's opinion
T	And?
Actor 2	And your opinion
T	What does your opinion count for here?
Mags	What does your opinion count for?
Actor 2	It destroyed more than people's livelihoods It destroyed the whole idea of the dignity of labour
Mags	Have these people paid to hear that?
Actor 2	No
T	Then what does it count for? I'm sorry, I didn't hear that

Actor 2 Nothing

Q I'd like an interval now, please

T We don't need an interval
Whoever ordered an interval they can cancel it

Mags There's too much to do

Q Don't you want an interval Prime Minister?

Mags *and* **T**
No

Pause.

Q There will now be a fifteen-minute interval

TEN: THE GAP

Actor 1 Are you going to tell them what you were telling me, back in the dressing room?

Actor 2 No

Actor 1 Why not?

Actor 2 I don't want to

Actor 1 What are you scared of?

Actor 2 I'm not scared

Actor 1 You're being a chicken

Actor 2 I'm not a chicken. What's history for you is life lived for me. It's not easy to talk about those years, not in public anyway

Actor 1 Go on, before they come back

Actor 2 My parents loved the Tories, I loathed them

Actor 1 Why in particular?

Actor 2 Well, you've seen Act One
It was their hypocrisy I hated most. For example – they allowed homophobia to thrive, whilst happily indulging in gay sex themselves. Section 28

Actor 1 What was that?

Actor 2 If I was to tell you, I'd be in breach of Section 28. An Orwellian piece of homophobic legislation, in the face of people dying from AIDS. Educating children about homosexuality was outlawed
Who are you playing in this half?

Actor 1 Michael Shea – he's the Queen's press secretary

Actor 2 I'm Rupert Murdoch – got a line of Prince Philip; look out for that one –

Actor 1 And I'm Kinnock

Actor 2 Are you?

Actor 1 Yes

Actor 2 I wanted to be Kinnock

Actor 1 Did you

Actor 2 I can do a good Kinnock

Actor 1 Yes but he's in my contract

Actor 2 Have you got his 'I warn you' speech?

Actor 1 No

Actor 2 Oh what a shame, you should have the 'I warn you' speech. It's bloody good

Actor 1 I know but he said it in '83

We've already gone past it

Actor 2 I warn you that you will have pain – when healing and relief depend upon payment

Actor 1 I'm Kinnock. You can't just take my part

Actor 2 I warn you that you will have ignorance – when learning is a privilege and not a right

Actor 1 I warn you that you will have poverty, when pensions slip –

Actor 2 And benefits are whittled away –

Actor 1 By a government that won't pay in an economy that can't pay

Actor 2 I warn you that you will be cold

Actor 1	When fuel charges are used as a tax system that the rich don't notice and the poor can't afford
Actor 2	I warn you that you must not expect work
Actor 1	I warn you not to go into the streets alone after dark
Actor 2	Or into the streets in large crowds of protest in the light
Actor 1	I warn you that you will be quiet
Actors 1 *and* **2**	When the curfew of fear and the gibbet of unemployment make you obedient
Actor 1	I warn you that you will borrow less – when credit, loans and mortgages are refused to people on your melting income

Mags and T have entered.

Actor 2	If Margaret Thatcher wins on Thursday, I warn you not to be ordinary
Actor 1	I warn you not to be young
Actor 2	I warn you not to fall ill
Actor 1	I warn you not to grow old
T	Denis

The actors notice T. Actor 2 puts Denis's glasses on.

Denis	Hello, love
T	Come away from him.
	Have you had some refreshments?
Denis	Yes, fully tanked up; ready for anything
Mags	Let us never forget this fundamental truth: the State has no source of money other than money

which people earn themselves. If the State wishes to spend, it can do so only by borrowing your savings or by taxing you more. It is no good thinking that someone else will pay – that 'someone else' is you. There is no such thing as public money; there is only taxpayers' money

Denis Well, there's the North Sea Oil and Gas money

And the money from all the public industries you're selling off

That's flooding the old coffers isn't it, Boss?

T Pardon?

Mags Don't try to pull the wool over my eyes

Denis

Never

Said any of that

Footman
Ladies and gentlemen

Pray be upstanding for Her Majesty the Queen

Q and Liz enter through the audience, shaking people's hands. Asking questions such as: 'Did you enjoy the interval?' 'Are you a regular theatregoer?' 'Do you live far away?' 'Very friendly staff here, don't you think?'

Q That was most enjoyable
We met everyone, all the stage management

Liz They went to such trouble

Q (*to Footman*) Thank you
Where are we?

T My second term, Your Majesty

Q	Oh yes
Mags	We were unleashing new forces in the land
T	Old orders everywhere were being questioned
Q	Great institutions
T	The NHS, the BBC, our universities and yes, the palace
Liz	It felt as if the palace and I had been shifted – Bottom priority in your Number 10
Q	We were told we had to provide value for money
Liz	I ask you – the Royal Family
Q	She started cancelling our meetings
T	They were always a distraction
Mags	One was pulled away from whatever one was doing And one was doing an awful lot

Mags curtsies.

Liz	I thought we might walk out in the grounds today, Prime Minister It's such a pleasant evening and the dogs could come
Mags	Of course, Your Majesty
T	A whole hour wasted in the chill And those dogs . . .
Liz	I was in Kenya when my father died. I remember sitting perfectly calmly feeling the future gaping before me
T	Why's she talking about this?

Liz	The local people were terribly kind. They simply lined the road as we drove back to Nairobi, heads bowed in respect
Mags	The whole Empire grieved for him
Liz	The press were wonderful too Not one camera was raised Not one photograph was taken; not one Their hats were off, to the last man
Mags	Really
Liz	Hard to believe now, isn't it?
Q	Michael, would you mind filling the young people in?
Shea	Not at all, Ma'am I'm Michael Shea, the Queen's press secretary I'm a Scot and I'll have a go at the accent. I have a background in diplomacy And I also write thrillers under a pseudonym Pretty good ones in fact –
Q	You can skip that
Shea	The tone of the press had changed towards the palace. In previous times, it had been universally reverential

Murdoch

The press had basically printed whatever fawning flummery the palace had given them. But I wasn't going to have that in my papers. I'm Rupert Murdoch, obviously.
When I bought *The Sun* in 1969 it was a soggy broadsheet. And I said to the editor – you're now part of a tabloid revolution. I want a tearaway paper with lots of tits in it

Q   We're talking about my family

Murdoch

In a minute
I wanted to buy *The Times* and *The Sunday Times*

T   Rupert was an ardent supporter in some very dark days

Murdoch

I snuck a meeting with Maggie down at Chequers. She helped me fly past the monopolies commission

Liz   Surely not

Q   She made a deal with him

Liz   That's utterly inappropriate

Q   Thirty years later it all came to light

Murdoch

Huge help in building my empire
All that claptrap about standards in journalism – Opinion, that's what people need

Q   It was the end of a quality paper

Liz   Prime Minister, I am worried about the pressure being put on my children – especially the Prince and Princess of Wales

Murdoch

Princess of Sales

Shea   Diana was hounded by the press wherever she went

Murdoch

Complained all the time – but she loved it too

Shea   I organised an informal lunch for the editors of the papers to meet the Queen, so that she might voice her concerns

Liz	It is hard on a girl if she can't even go to the local sweet shop without being cornered by photographers

Murdoch
Why couldn't she send a footman for the sweets?

Q	I think that is the most pompous remark I have ever heard in my life
Liz	Prime Minister, you have a better relationship with Mr Murdoch than I
Mags	Your Majesty, freedom of the press is one of the things upon which true democracy is founded
Liz	I quite agree
	But I must lay my family's predicament before you
	Surely we have a right to basic privacy
Q	This conversation never happened
We never walked in the garden
It would have been too hard on Mrs Thatcher's heels
Mags	Mr Murdoch may not be a monarchist
But the print unions have had their way too long
And he will take on the closed shop

Murdoch
If corporations ran things, we'd all be better off
I believe in as little government as possible

Mags	We have to trust business and industry to regulate itself
Liz	Then may one ask about the economy?
	Because it strikes one that the caps and the controls you have removed from our financial institutions

Mags The greater freedoms we have given

Liz Are widening the gap

T What gap?

Liz Between the rich and poor

Mags The country is getting richer. For the first time we have working-class people buying shares and owning homes

Liz But what about those who have lost their jobs? There are more children living in poverty than ever

Mags How can one relieve their poverty, unless it is by creating wealth? I know that socialists regard the pursuit of wealth as an evil, but right-minded people must surely see it as a good

Liz Not if the result is growing inequality.
And the culture that seems to be prevalent
This insatiable materialism –

T Has she forgotten she's the world's wealthiest woman?

Liz One sees these young men in the city really revelling in greed – lording it over the unemployed

T And there we have it. The true rise of the working class. My barrow boys in the city; that's what she can't brook

Mags I believe in the working class; not the shirking class

Q How can she reel off these ludicrous slogans to me?

T I didn't

Mags People remain poor because they know they will get state handouts

	We want to encourage them to get up, to seek work, to make money
Liz	Prime Minister, we've travelled a great deal this year As we do every year And the problem is not just in Britain. The poor are getting poorer And we have seen first hand The growing gap
T	It would be impolite to mention the fact that Her Majesty, Even as she championed the poor, Paid no tax until 1993 –
Liz	I had some very interesting talks with Mrs Gandhi on my visit to India recently and her view is that the uncontrolled free market is widening the gap –
Mags	With respect, Indira Gandhi was a radical Communist in her youth
T	The wealth created by a free economy will trickle down
Liz	Thank you for listening, Prime Minister
Denis	We had some smashing people down at Chequers for Christmas that year We had the Murdochs Jimmy Savile came – he's a laugh Joan Collins – if only Dear old Crawfie Carol And after the turkey we turned on the gogglebox for Her Maj
Liz	The greatest problem in the world today remains the gap between rich and poor countries
Mags	What?

Q	My Christmas broadcast
	Jolly good one that year
Liz	We can ignore the messages we don't like to hear
Mags	What's she talking about?
Liz	But we shall not begin to close this poverty gap until we hear less about nationalism and more about interdependence
Mags	That is quite wrong
Liz	One of the main aims of the Commonwealth is to make an effective contribution towards redressing the economic balance between nations
T	Denis
Mags	Denis, she's flouting our policies The entire British effort is to distance ourselves –
Liz	We in the Commonwealth are fortunate enough To belong to a worldwide comradeship
Mags, T *and* Denis	*Comradeship?*
Liz	Let us make the most of it Only then can we make the message of the angels come true: 'Peace on earth, goodwill towards men'
Mags	Good God
Liz	God bless you all
T	Is Her Majesty a socialist?
Denis	I don't think she's an actual Trot, old love
Mags	Then why, in her Christmas speech, is she expressing dubiously socialistic principles?

Q	They are in fact Christian principles And as Head of the Church One must freely express them
T	We were being undermined
Mags	Your Majesty, I'm sorry to tell you that your Christmas message has been interpreted, by some, as divergent to government policy
Liz	Really
Mags	It is your government's aim to reduce Commonwealth claims on the British taxpayer. Whatever your personal sentiments are, constitutionally you must ally yourself with your government
Liz	I have a duty to the Commonwealth as well as to my government
T	None of this was said This is all crass surmise
Liz	I vowed that duty before God. It is not something I can bend to / your convenience
Mags	If I may continue
Liz	You are asking me to / tear myself in two
Mags	If I may, your first duty
Liz	I have pledged a duty / as head of the Commonwealth
Mags	Your first duty is to the British people Not to a collection of nations Run by communists and mendicants
T	I never said that
Liz	She cut me off She actually cut me off

Q	Attila the hen
	I think that was Denis Healey
Liz	Who called her the Maggietollah?
Q	One had to laugh
T	The palace found our fervour for improvement funny. It was hurtful
Liz	You held the Commonwealth in contempt And that attitude trickled down
Q	The new free market wealth did not

ELEVEN: BOMBS II

Liz	I was in the United States on a private visit to inspect some American studs
	When the news came that a bomb had exploded at the Conservative Party conference in Brighton
Q	When any great disaster happens where there is loss of life
	One feels a physical sense of dread
Liz	It was hard to get accurate news at first No one knew how many casualties there were – or whom
Mags	It was three a.m. I was putting the finishing touches to the next day's speech, when
T	The second it happened I thought
	I'm amazed this hasn't happened before
Mags	The noise
	Windows blown to smithereens I thought Denis

T	It was like an earthquake
Denis	Margaret
Mags	But the lights stayed on
T	In the corridor, people were thrown against walls
	The bathroom gone in a cloud of dust
Mags	One always imagines that one will be plunged into darkness at a moment like that
	But the lights stayed on
T	I was still in my evening gown from the night before. Had I been in that bathroom I would not have . . .
Mags	I would have . . .
T	We were very lucky
Denis	Put your speech in the bag
	If it's in your handbag it won't get lost
Q	There were five dead,
	Others with terrible injuries
	Four floors of the hotel had collapsed
T	It was an attempt to destroy, to cripple, to wipe out Her Majesty's democratically elected government. That is the scale of the outrage
Liz	When I was eventually put through
	Before I could even speak
	Mrs Thatcher said
Mags	Are you having a wonderful time?
Q	Wasn't that strange? Wasn't that a peculiar response?
	Such bizarre forced jollity
	At a moment like that

Liz	Margaret, are you all right?
Mags	Yes thank you. We are fine
Liz	You must be experiencing very deep shock
Mags	Of course one isn't thinking of oneself One is thinking of the injured And the victims
Liz	Of course Have they given you lots of tea? Tea is terribly good for shock
Q	I didn't know what else to say
Mags	I am perfectly, perfectly fine and untouched
Liz	Philip and I are watching images as they come through on the news It is dreadful
Mags	Thank you so much for your kind concern. There's a Marks and Spencer's
Liz	Pardon?
Mags	We're sending out to Marks and Spencer's We need clothes They're helping us with all the delegates who came out in pyjamas And we're going on
Liz	Are you?
Mags	With the conference. We're going on
Q	We watched her speech the next day Not a hair out of place
Liz	She made reference to the atrocity and then she just carried on
Mags	The fact that we are gathered here now, shocked but composed and determined, is a sign that not

	only has this attack failed but that all attempts to destroy democracy through terrorism will fail
Q	Profoundly impressive But at what cost?
Denis	After Brighton, I started thinking she should look to an end You know, towards getting out
Q	Two weeks later, Indira Ghandi was assassinated outside her own home
Liz	Mrs Thatcher brought me the news
Mags	It wasn't terrorists or strangers. It was two of her own personal guards
Liz	Good God
Mags	One of them discharged three rounds into her abdomen. And then his accomplice opened fire on her as she lay on the ground
Q	They removed thirty bullets from her body
Liz	She feared that something like this might happen
Mags	One does fear it, doesn't one
T	No, no it wasn't fear that I felt; it wasn't fear
Q	It's not fear exactly. One just knows it could be over – that quickly
Liz	If I die a violent death – the violence will be in the thought of my assassin, not in my dying
Mags	Who said that?
Liz	Indira
	She knew One cannot make so many enemies And not know

T	It was her own – her own trusted men that did it That's what I could not brook
Liz	Are you all right?
Mags	After Brighton the IRA said Today we were unlucky But remember, we only have to be lucky once You will have to be lucky always
Q	Yes; it was chilling
Mags	The hatred in it And the number of people The number of people in this country who Who wish they had got me
Liz	I'm sure that can't be true
Mags	Well, they didn't get me I am not that easy to dispose of And as long as there is breath in my body I will
Liz	Would you like a scone, Prime Minister?
Mags	Thank you
T	Denis bought me a watch Unusual gesture of affection Engraved on it is 'Every minute counts' I won't waste one of them
Liz	The jam is home-made There's damson and that one's bilberry
Q	I didn't say that We never have bilberry jam
Liz	One likes to support the village fetes around Sandringham One's always buying little jars at local sales of work

Mags	I think one's always looking for the jam that tastes like home. No one made jam like my mother could. She was very much a woman of the home and I can remember the smell of her gooseberry like it was yesterday
Liz	I don't think there's a woman of our whole generation who can't make jam
Q	And marmalade
Mags	We all learnt from the homily of housekeeping And I still believe it would save many a financier from failure
Liz	You see sometimes it could almost be nice

TWELVE: WET WET WET

T	Wets
Mags	Do you know what a 'wet' is?
T	My backbench was full of them
Mags	Etonians, the old guard
T	They didn't like the taste of my reforming medicine
Mags	They looked down on me for being lower class
Q	Anyone who disagreed with her was branded wet
T	I knew the enemy across the floor in the House The Left
Mags *and* T	Kinnochio
Mags	I had that enemy in my sights Where I could squeeze and pulverise it

T	But another enemy began to appear
Q	She changed after Brighton
Mags *and* **T**	Wets
Q	One spoke with people in her own party and the feeling was that she was rather cutting herself off
T	These were often the old grandees Dripping with titles, land and wealth Not like Norman Tebbit and me
Mags	Wets and ultra wets
T	Spineless
Q	One sees it again and again The longer a leader serves The less open they become
Mags	Our monarch I'm sorry to tell you Is wet
T	We never said that
Liz	For a Methodist, she's remarkably unchristian
Q	We never said *that*
Liz	One wondered if she was a religious person
Q	No, one didn't
Liz	Yes, one did One talked about it with the Archbishop
Q	Oh yes
Liz	He felt sure she had faith but he wasn't sure that the doctrine of grace meant much to her
Howe	Geoffrey Howe, Foreign Secretary. I wasn't a wet

Mags Yes you were

Howe No I wasn't, Margaret. I was one of your own
I sat by your side
And I must say I heard one question more and more often

Mags Is he one of us?

T Whose side is he on?

Howe About people in our own party

Mags Sometimes I think you're dripping, Geoffrey
A big wet sheep

Q She bullied poor Geoffrey terribly

Howe I think one of the things that you never fully absorbed, Margaret, is that it's bad management as well as bad manners to reproach as it were officers in front of other ranks

Mags *and* **T**
 Oh dear

Howe If you want to tick people off or have arguments with them then you should, as a matter of courtesy, do it in private

Mags You are Foreign Secretary. Foreign affairs are interesting, Geoffrey – they are interesting! And your endless drone has the whole cabinet comatose

Howe You are becoming increasingly reckless, if you like, of the way in which you conduct your personal relationships

Mags Go and tell Crawfie I'm ready for my comb-out

T To be wet is to be like a soggy August

 The whole concept reminded me of Balmoral

Q	I'm sorry to tell you that Mrs Thatcher didn't care for Balmoral
T	Bagpipes
	Wellingtons Torment
Q	She came for three days every year like all my PMs
Liz	Harold Wilson brought his dogs We always had a jolly time
Mags	I said Crawfie, pack something warm For heaven's sake pack thermals
Liz	We love throwing on a headscarf and striding over the moors
	And we especially love our picnics
T	It's an unnerving experience
	Prince Philip cooking drumsticks under damp tarpaulins Eating with Tupperware on the side of a windblown hill
Liz	Would you like the gherkins, Mrs Thatcher?
Mags	I'll get them Let me serve them Let me pass them round Your Royal Highness, would you like a gherkin?
Liz	She kept on jumping up to help But we enjoy serving people at our picnics
Mags	It completely dismayed me
T	The Queen, rolling up her sleeves to rinse the mugs
Mags	Let me do that, Your Majesty, I'm a dab hand with the washing-up – let me

Q	Philip said
Philip	Someone tell that bloody woman to sit down
T	It was more stressful than a NATO summit
Q	I know our life up there does not appeal to everyone But it is home And when one opens it to guests
Liz	She used to leave at six in the morning Really as soon as she could One found it rude
Q	Hurtful
Shea	Michael Shea again Mrs Thatcher's style became ever more regal She began to use the royal 'we'
Mags	I am not an 'I did this, I did that' person. I have never been an 'I' person. I prefer to talk about 'we' – the government . . . it is not I who do things, it is we, the government
T	We have become a grandmother
Q	Have you come to talk about 1986?
Shea	Yes I have
Q	I expect a lot of you were not yet born Or still at school Or listening to those dreadful bands Diana used to like
Shea	In 1986
T	Prince Andrew got married to Sarah Ferguson. A lovely wedding
Q	He looked kingly

Shea I wasn't going to talk about that

Liz The press called her an unbrushed red setter trying to get out of a potato sack. I thought that was a bridge too far

T The Queen's trooping horse Burmese retired after seventeen years

Shea I wasn't going to talk about that either

T Well, what else are you qualified to talk about?

Shea I was going to talk about your decision to allow America to bomb Libya, using Britain as its base

T The Queen has no wish to discuss that

Q Yes I do

   She let Reagan send his planes from our airbases

Liz It broke international law and it had terrible repercussions

Actor 2 There was an all-time hullaballoo in the house. I would like to remind the Right Honourable Lady –

Actor 1 Who are you being?

Actor 2 Kinnock

Actor 1 I'm Kinnock

Actor 2 You're Michael Shea

Actor 1 I can be Kinnock and Shea

Actor 2 Then don't miss your chance

Actor 1 (*as Kinnock*) I would like to remind the Right Honourable Lady that the hullaballoo came not just from the Labour Party but from her own back benches, from her own cabinet

T	You're not Kinnock
Kinnock	Would the Right Honourable Lady agree that there is only one reason why President Reagan sought her cooperation?
T	You're not anybody
Kinnock	The President knew that when he said jump, she would reply how high?
Q	(*to Actor 1*) Would you be Michael Shea again, please? I think you were about to mention South Africa
Shea	I was about to mention South Africa
Q	Thank you
Shea	The international community was putting pressure on Great Britain to impose sanctions on the apartheid regime
Mags	Britain will not be imposing sanctions on South Africa
Liz	But the Commonwealth has made a pledge to eradicate apartheid
Mags	Ma'am, the ANC is a Marxist Leninist organisation –
Liz	Apartheid, Prime Minister Now, we fought against the Nazis And I can see no difference
Mags	Were the ANC to take power, South Africa would be plunged into socialist chaos / and the economy –
Liz	The Commonwealth's position is clear Apartheid is *out*

Mags First, anyone who thinks the ANC can form a government is living in cloud cuckoo land –

Liz That's up to the people. Don't forget what you learnt in Zimbabwe

Mags Secondly, to impose sanctions
Would not only plunge the poor into further poverty
It would be a hindrance to British trade

Ron And American trade
Margaret and I, yet again we shared a vision . . .
You know, I attempted to veto US sanctions
But can you believe it?
I was overridden by Congress

T I had Ron's personal support if not his government's

Ron It was the first time this century that any president was overruled on foreign policy

T Why did they not see that we were right?

Ron Margaret, we were just too far ahead sometimes

T Oh, Ron

Q She wouldn't listen. She stuck with her opinion

Liz Alone in the UN, alone in the Commonwealth, in the commons

Q Alone in her own cabinet

Howe Geoffrey Howe again. The resignations had begun. Michael Heseltine went

T Jolly good riddance, I say

Howe I think, Margaret, that he felt his views weren't being listened to. I wish I had some Heseltine lines to convey his indignation but I haven't

T	He threw quite a tantrum – stormed out of cabinet with a flick of his hair
Howe	Then Leon Brittan went, Nigel Lawson. And when Willie Whitelaw retired, Margaret lost her best restraining influence
T	Every Prime Minister needs a Willie
Howe	She became more and more reliant on her unelected advisers. They had her ear and she wouldn't listen to her own ministers –
Mags	You are interrupting a scene. The Queen is about to speak
Howe	Beg pardon, Your Majesty
Mags	You haven't even got the correct year. Willy retired in '87 and we are still in '86
Howe	Oh
Mags	Why don't you stop bleating until you have your facts right?
Liz	One sees Black South Africans seeking basic human rights Being violently oppressed – Surely this is this very thing That you abhor in Communist countries The utter lack of freedom And the brutal state control?
Mags	The political science here Is quite different
Q	So patronising
Liz	There comes a time When morally One must say no The Commonwealth is demanding sanctions

Mags	I welcome your point of view I value your advice.
	Thank you for the tea-cake, Your Majesty

THIRTEEN: BREAKFAST AT HOLYROOD

Q	One suspects she is racist
T	I am not a racist, I am NOT What I feel about the Black South Africans Is exactly the same as I feel about the Germans The Italians, the Greeks Or anyone else not blessed to be British
Shea	Michael Shea again The Commonwealth Games were held in Edinburgh that year The opening ceremony was spectacular Five thousand children in a human mosaic
Liz	But Michael, thirty-two nations have boycotted in protest Hardly an African country there – because of her intransigence on sanctions
Shea	The games were indeed looking very White
Liz	It cannot be borne. It simply cannot
Shea	Something had to be done Of course I didn't do it I didn't do anything at all
	Mags and Liz open newspapers.
	On July the twentieth, *The Sunday Times* Announced Her Majesty's dismay At the policies of the government

T	It was a huge, huge spread
Q *and* T	Pages
Shea	The journalists Michael Jones, political editor And Simon Freeman (backstabbing bastard) Claimed irrefutable evidence That the Queen found her Prime Minister
T	Uncaring, confrontational and socially divisive
Shea	It was very precise
T	The journalists said the Queen was fully aware it would be published
Shea	Here are the bullet points: One:
Liz	One feared that the suppression of the miners' strike had done long-term damage to the fabric of the state
Shea	Two:
Liz	One objected to America's bombing raids on Libya departing from British airbases
Shea	Three:
Liz	One supported sanctions in South Africa and abhorred apartheid
Shea	Four:
Liz	One had deep concerns about our own disintegrating race relations and inner-city decay
Shea	And that overall
Liz	One felt the whole direction of government policy was –
T	What a betrayal

Q	Never said it Never wrote it Nothing to do with me
T	For an unelected monarch To oppose the government – Unconstitutional and dangerous
Shea	Ironically we were together when the news broke One of the rare occasions I was with them both The Queen The Prime Minister and myself At Holyrood in Edinburgh It was breakfast time

Mags and Liz are both reading the revelations.

Shea	Well I couldn't eat a thing The silence was so sickening
T	I didn't trust myself to speak I wasn't angry; it's not that. I was surprised
Q	It was her friend Mr Murdoch's paper I felt like leaping up and saying there There you are This is what it's like when the papers turn on you No one is safe from a ruthless press
Shea	The Prime Minister's face was quite unmoving
Liz	Well One wonders how this happened, Michael
Shea	I'd like to apologise Profusely to you both Your Majesty Prime Minister Yes it's true I did meet Simon Freeman And we were talking off the record

| | Quite informally
And he asked about the Commonwealth
I replied that as head of the Commonwealth
The Queen ...
Is naturally very keen on it
And so forth |
|---|---|

> The rest is all his supposition
> Prime Minister, I can assure you that
> I had no briefing with Her Majesty
>
> The Queen had no prior knowledge of this article
> And indeed
> I have never, ever heard her
> Speaking critically of you
> Or any of her previous Prime Ministers

Shea	Mrs Thatcher said only three words to me:
Mags	Never mind, dear
Shea	That was it
T	Never mind, dear
Shea	It was the most excruciating breakfast I was ever at

Pause.

| T | I was knocked sideways
I was very, very down |
|---|---|
| Liz | Margaret
I'm sorry this has happened |
| Mags | Thank you, Ma'am

Really I am so respectful |
| Liz | That is mutual, you know |

FOURTEEN: THE WORLD WON'T LISTEN

Q	The President of the United States
	May only serve for two terms
Liz	No matter how powerful one's allies are, they are passing
	There is no permanence in politics
Q	I've spent a lifetime in the ebb and flow of power
	It brings its gifts
	But then it's an intoxicant
	One must beware lest one consumes too much
T	We tried to advise and assist George Bush as we had Ron, but he didn't seem so
Mags	He didn't have Ron's friendly personality
	And sadly we disagreed over Germany
T	No one but me could see the threat of reunification
Mags	We've beaten the Germans twice and we don't want them back
Howe	Her attitude to Europe confounded me. It was blinkered by prejudice
T	Are you back, Geoffrey? You'd better have something worthwhile to say
Howe	European unity strengthens our position in world, improves our prospects for economic success –
Mags	Oh bla bla bla
Howe	Together, the nations of Europe can work towards global objectives, which no single member state can achieve on its own

Mags	We have not rolled back the frontiers of the State in Britain only to see them reimposed at a European level
Howe	She could undo the careful work of a whole conference with a single utterance
Mags	No No NO
Clarke	Kenneth Clarke, Education Secretary Margaret began to believe her own propaganda; she began to fly by the seat of her pants. She began to get more scratchy. And the poll tax; what a disaster. Geoffrey, explain what it was, would you? I have to be Kinnock
Howe	Margaret felt the rating system put too much pressure on homeowners, so the poll tax, or community charge –
T	If Geoffrey explains we'll still be here at breakfast time tomorrow
Kinnock	The community charge is the most flagrantly unjust taxation we have seen since the peasant's revolt in 1381
T	The community charge is the flagship of the Thatcher fleet. I can defend it clearly, explicitly, at any time, in any place and to any person
Liz	So how does it work then?
Mags	It is designed to prevent overspending left-wing councils from squeezing homeowners any further. Everyone pays the same
Liz	A bus driver in his council flat pays the same as the Duke of Westminster in his mansion – have I got that correct?

Mags Yes. And you, Ma'am, pay nothing at all

Kinnock It is fundamentally unfair, costly and crushing to families

Howe Margaret thought her will alone could push it through – but she got the mood of the people wrong

Q The people didn't think her tax was fair
They refused to pay it – and they rioted

Protestor
No, they demonstrated

Mags They were anarchists and scum

Protestor
Two hundred thousand citizens marched peacefully up Whitehall

Mags The rabble set Trafalgar Square on fire. The looting and rampaging, violence and destruction went on for hours

T I was brought up to respect law and order

Protestor
The police blocked both ends of Whitehall, so the crowd couldn't disperse. Then, with no warning, they sent in the riot squad

Mags We are moving on

Protestor
No we're not.

I am protesting.

By three o clock, the police had corralled us into Trafalgar Square. How to turn citizens into a mob? Charge at them on horses. Drive through them in riot vans at high speed. Fear makes you defend yourself; it is incendiary. Demonstrators

	became rioters and on that day, the act of protest was made criminal
Howe	I feared her flagship was sinking
T	I was brought up by a Victorian grandmother
Mags	You were taught to respect law and order, to work jolly hard, to improve yourself, you were taught self-reliance, you lived within your income
T	You were patriotic, you had self-respect, you were a good member of your community
Mags	These things are Victorian values
Howe	She was losing her touch. Opinion polls were very low. By-elections disastrous
T	In the cabinet I could almost hear knives being sharpened
Q	It's rare for a leader to know when to go
Mags	I will go on to win a fourth term and a fifth – as long as the people want me and Britain needs me
Howe	I knew when to go

This is my resignation speech |
| Q | Not all of it, Geoffrey, please |
| Howe | I'll cut the references to cricket, Ma'am

The conflict of loyalty, of loyalty to my Right Honourable Friend the Prime Minister and of loyalty to what I perceive to be the true interests of the nation, has become all too great |
| Mags | His was a slow poison |
| Howe | I no longer believe it possible to resolve that conflict from within this Government. That is why I have resigned |

Mags	That quiet voice of his
Howe	The time has come for others to consider their own response to the tragic conflict of loyalties with which I have myself wrestled for perhaps too long
T	He gave them permission to revolt
Liz	Philip showed me a cartoon from *The Times* the next day. It was of Geoffrey Howe as a huge sheep, swallowing Mrs Thatcher whole – just her heels sticking out. A caption read 'Howe's That?'
Mags	I will call their bluff
T	Flush the traitors out
Mags	If they want a leadership challenge By golly I'll give them one
T	I'm a world stateswoman
Mags	On the verge of committing our troops to Kuwait
T	I'm a proven election winner
Mags	And I can count on my party to back me to the hilt
T	When someone says you have a contest, you do not run away, you fight it
Mags	Come on, boys Let's have a leadership challenge Who's up to it? Who thinks that they can take me on?
Heseltine	I've been waiting years for this
T	The mighty Heseltine
Heseltine	I've sat long enough on the back benches
Mags	Festering

Heseltine
>Watching as you've estranged the brightest and the best in your cabinet. You never appreciated our contribution and you take credit for all our triumphs

T   It's all about you, isn't it, Michael?

Heseltine
>This party would have got on just as well and achieved just as much without you, Margaret

Mags   That is preposterous

Heseltine
>They say a man should be judged by his enemies
>I am very proud of mine

T   Tarzan stood against me

Heseltine
>I am the man to lead Britain into the 1990s

FIFTEEN: DIAMONDS ARE FOREVER

Mags   I was in Paris for the first vote
Bush, Mitterrand, Gorbachev, Kohl
They were all there

T   I was advised to stay in London and canvass people in the Commons tea room. I ask you. I was Prime Minister

Mags   The vote was counted as I was signing one of the treaties that ended the Cold War. Denis phoned me through the news

Denis   You did very well, old love. You didn't lose. But forty per cent of your own party voted against you

T   Ever so slightly, the ground shifted under my feet

Mags	I'm going forward, Denis I will make the party rally In my hour of need they'll come back to me
Denis	I knew then she was done for
T	That night, Crawfie and I stayed up. We talked
Mags	Grantham
T	School
Mags	The horrible headmistress who attempted to thwart my ambition
T	Oxford
Mags	How they tried to look down on me
T	Denis
Mags	My twins
T	The way I would often forget to wave up at the nursery window on my way to work
Mags	I was so busy you see
T	As dawn came we were still talking
Mags	We didn't go to bed at all
Liz	At our audience on her return, the Prime Minister told me she'd contest a second ballot
Mags	I shall carry on batting for Britain, with all the vigour and energy I have
Q	What could one say? They'd scuttled her. She was slowly sinking
Liz	As a human being, one always has hope
Clarke	Kenneth Clarke. Margaret said she wanted to see us, one by one. I was first in

Mags   Kenneth, can I count on your support?

Clarke   Look, Margaret, this whole process is farcical. It's time to go. Do you really want to see Michael Heseltine Prime Minister? It's time to clear the field for Douglas Hurd or Major; someone who can win

T   At least Kenneth Clarke stabbed me in the front

Mags   A dismal procession followed.

T   Old school ties and sweating brows. One of them even cried

Tory 1   I am on your side

Tory 2   You know you have my loyalty

Tory 1   But honestly?

Tory 2   I don't think any of the others

Tory 1   The support just isn't there

T   The message was clear

Tory 1 *and* Tory 2
    You will never win

Mags   I considered you my friends and allies and it disgusts me that with your weasel words you have transmuted your betrayal into frank advice. It sickens me that you pretend concern for my fate. Because this is treachery. It is treachery with a smile on its face

    I have won three elections and I could go on without you. By God I have deserved it. I've done everything for years. Not one of you could have achieved one tenth

Denis   Margaret
Give it up
Give it up, old girl
Come on

Mags I am not a quitter
I am not a quitter

Denis Let it go

Pause. Actor 2 exits.

T And so
The following morning I went once more to my cabinet

Mags And I stood down
As their leader
As Prime Minister
It was the only thing to do

T I then telephoned world leaders

Mags There was utter disbelief

T Bush said some very gracious things
And then he asked about my successor

Mags I was already history

Q Mrs Thatcher sat where she had sat in every audience for the last eleven years. She told me she was going to stand down

Liz That must have been a very difficult decision

Mags You don't take a decision like that without it being difficult
Without there being heartbreak
Yes, there is heartbreak
But it is the right thing

Liz Mrs Thatcher's emotion was not perceptible in anything she said. Her effort to contain it was remarkable

Q It was the same for me when our Royal Yacht *Britannia* was decommissioned. I was resolutely determined that no tears would be seen to fall

Liz	The last few days must have been traumatic for you
Mags	Yes But we got through them And tonight we will leave Number 10 for the
T	For the last time
Liz	Would you like a whisky?
Mags	Thank you, Ma'am
Liz	I shall have my Gin and It
	One tries to keep everything together One does one's very best But sometimes the harder one holds on, the more things fall apart. I fear there are some tricky times ahead
Mags	For you, Ma'am?
Liz	My children are all unhappy If they had privacy they might have found a private solace but There is a crisis brewing, Margaret. Charles and Diana cannot reconcile And I won't have divorce I will not, cannot have it
Liz	Here's to certainty
All	To certainty
	They drink.
Mags	I hope that in my years at Number 10 I have done what I set out to do
Liz	You have achieved a great deal; that, no one can deny
Mags	I set out to change the soul of this country

Q	How very disturbing
Liz	And now, where will you go?
Mags	To the back benches I won't shirk it I'll confound them all
Q	You always have
T	And when I'm out of politics, I'm going to run a shop. It'll be called Rent-A-Spine
Liz	Where will you live?
Mags	We've a house in Dulwich Denis chose it Spanking new Right next to his golf course On the South Circular
Liz	I'm sure it will be an exciting new chapter
Mags	It will never happen to you, Your Majesty
Liz	I'm sorry?
Mags	You will never relinquish your power
Liz	But Prime Minister In our democracy I have none
Q	How do you do? How do you do?
T	We regard the Royal Family as the greatest asset Britain has. They are a focus of patriotism, loyalty, affection and esteem.
Liz	When one sees you in the House And hears them baying at you One can't imagine how you keep your poise

	They really are so dreadful Like an awful pack of schoolboys
Mags	Yes they can be odious But I thrive on it you see I stand out in my blue and blonde And I thrive
Liz	Quite so
Mags	Without it I'm not sure what I will do
Q	That afternoon, she took Prime Minister's Questions in the House. We watched her on the television
Liz	Her performance was pure Iron Lady
Mags	The Berlin Wall has been torn down and the Cold War is at an end. These immense changes didn't come about by chance. They have been achieved by resolution in defence – and by a refusal ever to be intimidated. And all these things were done in teeth of the opposition of the Right Honourable Gentlemen opposite – and their ladies

Should we be censured for our strength?

Mags exits.

Footman 1
The atmosphere on the street is amazing, Ma'am. There are people dancing out there, shouting 'She's gone, she's gone'

Liz	Really

Footman 2
Absolute jubilation

Actor 1	Do you remember it?

Actor 2   We partied for days. It was wonderful. A tremendous feeling that anything could happen
          That

Actor 1   That what?

Actor 2   That things could only get better

          Actor 1 and 2 exit.

Liz   It is affecting when they go
          One doesn't have time to turn around
          Out goes the last and in comes the next with barely a pause
          And one has often built up a relationship

          Liz exits.

Q   Of course stories about clashes

T   Nonsense

Q   There was never any question

T   Stories about clashes

Q   There was never a rift

T   We have always loved the Queen

Q   The Baroness read out the eulogy when Ronald Regan died
          It was impeccable

T   We here still move in twilight
          But we have a beacon to guide us
          We have his example
          Let us give thanks for a life that achieved so much for all of God's children

Q   I would have put it slightly differently

          The fortieth president
          Like Michael Shea our dear press secretary
          Died of dementia

T	One doesn't die of dementia, Ma'am It is not a fatal condition One dies of something else. One lives with dementia

They are both standing.

Q	Won't you sit down?

Pause.

T	No

The End.